INTERFAITH PILGRIMS
LIVING TRUTHS AND TRUTHFUL LIVING

ELEANOR NESBITT

SWARTHMORE LECTURE 2003

QUAKER *Q* BOOKS

First published in May 2003 by Quaker Books
Friends House, Euston Road, London NW1 2BJ

http://www.quaker.org.uk

ISBN 0 85245 347 7

Design & typesetting: Jonathan Sargent
Printed and bound in Great Britain by Biddles Ltd www.biddles.co.uk
Text typeface: Venetian 301, 13 on 15pt

We thank Caroline Jariwala for permission to reproduce her painting *Krishnalila* (2002), the original is mixed media on canvas 48" x 48".
We also thank the following copyright holders for permission to reproduce material: The Friend Publications Ltd for extracts from Adams 2000 and Albright 1999. Kamil Muslim Trust for Islamic Propagation Centre, Qatar, for extracts from Ali (1946). Oxford Diocesan Committee for Interfaith Concerns for extracts from Boulter (2001) and Bowker (2001). World Congress of Faiths, Oxford, for extract from Braybrooke (2002). Redbridge SACRE for extract from Copley (1998). Kenneth Cragg for extract from The Call of the Minaret. Extract reprinted on p.76 from Amritvela by Leena Dhingra, published in 1988 in Great Britain by The Women's Press Ltd, 34 Great Sutton Street, London EC1V 0LQ, is used by permission of The Women's Press Ltd. Beacon Press, Boston for extract from Diana Eck, Encountering God (1993). Extract from Farid Esack, Qu'ran, Liberation and Pluralism, © Farid Esack, 1997, reproduced by permission of Oneworld Publishers. Cambridge University Press for extract from David Ford, Self and Salvation (1999). Navajivan Trust, Ahmedabad 380014, India for Gandhi (1927 and 1928). Penguin Books Ltd for extracts from Mascaró (1965). BFSS National RE Centre, Isleworth, for extract from Morgan (1989). Saraswati Press, Allahabad, for extract from Premchand, Mansarovar. Continuum International Publishing Group Ltd for extract from Jonathan Sacks, The Dignity of Difference (2002). UAHC Press, New York, for extract from Schindler (1988). Harper Collins, San Francisco, for extracts from Singh (1995). Paul Vallely and The Independent for extract from Vallely (2002). Pantheon Books, New York, for extract from Zimmer (1946).

PREFACE

The Swarthmore Lectureship was established by the Woodbrooke Extension Committee at a meeting held December 9, 1907: the minute of the Committee providing for an 'annual lecture on some subject relating to the message and work of the Society of Friends'. The name Swarthmore was chosen in memory of the home of Margaret Fox, which was always open to the earnest seeker after Truth, and from which loving words of sympathy and substantial material help were sent to fellow workers.

The lectureship has a twofold purpose: first, to interpret to the members of the Society of Friends their message and mission; and secondly, to bring before the public the spirit, the aims and fundamental principles of Friends. The lecturers alone are responsible for any opinions expressed.

The lectureship provides both for the publication of a book and for the delivery of a lecture, the latter usually at the time of assembly of Britain Yearly Meeting of the Society of Friends. A lecture related to the present book was delivered at Yearly Meeting in London on the evening of May 3, 2003.

The Swarthmore Lecture Committee can be contacted via the Clerk, c/o Woodbrooke, 1046 Bristol Road, Selly Oak, Birmingham B29 6LJ.

DEDICATION

For my father, the Revd W. Ralph Nesbitt,
and my mother, Martha ('Pattie') Nesbitt,
who showed me such different ways of
believing and understanding,
in loving memory…

CONTENTS

ACKNOWLEDGEMENTS

My heart is full of thanks and these acknowledgements cannot hope to pay adequate tribute. That being said, I thank the Swarthmore Lecture Committee – in particular Pam Lunn as an inspirational, supportive and meticulous critic and friend and Geoffrey Carnall and Helen Carmichael for their wise guidance. My thanks go to staff at Woodbrooke Quaker Study Centre for their hospitality in 2002. I thank those who inspired me in Cambridge's Jesus Lane Meeting long ago, and I thank Coventry PM for many, many friendships over the past 25 years. I am grateful to the University of Warwick for study leave in 2002 and for the opportunities to learn from my students and colleagues. Thank you to my friends from different communities of faith – especially Hazel Green and Kamla Sawhney – and to friends including Rex Ambler, Hugh Boulter, Lesley Butterwick, Ann Henderson, Karima Imtiaz, Julia Leslie, Colin McKenzie, Peggy Morgan, Alan Race and May Youett for helping me to improve what I had drafted. My husband, Ram Krishan, has been a constant source of strength and insight, with an uncanny knack of finding material germane to whatever I happen to be writing at that moment. Any mistakes are mine, and I will be glad to have my attention drawn to them.

NOTES ON THE TEXT

In this book BCE (Before the Common Era) and CE (Common Era) are used in preference to BC and AD. This is the accepted practice in religious studies.

I have followed the convention of inserting references in the text so that any interested reader can (via the list of references at the end of the book) trace publications which relate to a particular point. Internet webpage details were accurate when accessed in November 2002.

Quotations from the Bible are from the Revised Standard Version.

A number of words from other languages appear in the text. The way in which the roman alphabet is used by speakers of English is not phonetically consistent, and there are several ways in which such words can appear in the roman alphabet. I have tried to use transliterations that are acceptable to scholars (eg Makkah for Mecca), but have omitted the extra dots and dashes (diacritical marks) which some writers use. Specialists will realise what marks have been omitted.

CHAPTER ONE

Setting the Scene

Love the truth more than all.
(George Fox, Epistle 65 in Ambler 2001: 16)
Yet every Truth is true in its kind.
(Isaac Penington, *Quaker faith & practice* 27.22)

How this book will unfold

This book is the response to a challenge from the Swarthmore
Lecture Committee to give 'a lecture on interfaith issues,
looking at questions of what truth is and how different truths
relate and talk to one another'. I hope that my response will
encourage us all in our joyful and creative adventuring towards
truth. Quakers were 'Friends of Truth' before they were Friends
(Punshon 1990: 65ff), so we have a particular interest in
truth! I shall share moments of my own journey in the hope
that they may prompt readers to reflect on their own stories.
My own experience is one of new insights dawning intermit-
tently and of a path which seems to ascend only gradually as it
makes its way up the slopes. To mix metaphors even more, this
book shares some patches of a quilt, some stones from a mosaic,
rather than offering a neatly constructed argument or a mounting crescendo. Some of the patches (or pieces of the mosaic)

appear close up, as if they are under a magnifying glass, others will appear in less detail. This is true to how life has unfurled for me and my hope is that what I have written will connect with you: I realise that different points will connect with different readers.

Chapter one sets the scene, and this includes explaining my own background, so that you can understand my account in its particular context. I shall go on to suggest that we increasingly experience our society as plural, 'multifaith', post-modern and fast-changing, a world in which old certainties are dissolving whilst (and with the result that) our need for assurance is greater than ever before. Some individuals' knee-jerk reaction to this evident diversity is to take refuge in 'fundamentalism' of one type or another. It is these believers' absolute truths, and their manner of proclaiming them and denouncing any other point of view, which may be hardest for those of us who are tentative seekers and liberals to come to terms with. At the individual level too, I shall suggest, we are in some sense plural – because we are travellers who are changed by our journey.

As our travel has a spiritual intention we are also pilgrims – and chapter two begins by exploring this metaphor. It suggests useful publications for interfaith pilgrims and recommends that we become aware of the many 'dimensions' of what we call religion. We also have to ask ourselves what we mean by 'other faiths', and – more fundamentally – what we mean by 'other'. And we have to acknowledge that we bring ourselves to each encounter, and that each encounter in turn affects what we are.

In chapter three we shall be considering the 'lenses', including our Quaker lens, through which we look at the world. For instance, the very language that we inherit as a medium for our ruminations and discussions makes it likely that as speakers of English we will envisage truth differently from, say, speakers of Mandarin. I will emphasise the need to be alert to our neighbour's actual concerns (rather than what we presuppose them to be). Moreover, by introducing some concepts from India's religious vocabulary, I hope to make the point that it is through trying to understand another person's concepts that we become more deeply aware of who we are, and of our own conditioning. It is of course also a way into a deeper understanding of our neighbour.

Worship is the focus of chapter four, because we can catch sight of truth in both the spontaneity and the unfamiliar conventions of our neighbours' worship. After sharing something of Hindu worship, we will look enquiringly at the possibility of interfaith worship, and wonder whether our Meetings for Worship are in some sense already interfaith.

It is in chapter five that we turn to the matter of what we mean by truth. We will consider the notions of truth that are embedded in and expressed through our faith traditions and communities, and we will look at the human drive to arrive at just one truth or one formulation of it. We ask: Do all faiths have creeds? What does oneness mean? Does it mean the same thing as being unique? Can claims to the uniqueness of a revelation sit alongside an awareness of plurality? I shall suggest that we embrace truth as paradox, because this can free us up for engaging imaginatively with the faith of others.

'Betruthal' (not 'betrothal') is the title of the final chapter: truth involves us in turning, facing and engaging. It means exercising discernment as well as making a leap of love. I shall reaffirm our approach to truth as an engagement with what is live and active: an engagement requiring us to be steadfast in keeping our troth/truth.

Orienting ourselves

Four quotations provide a preliminary context for what is to follow. First, from a Hindu seeker, who lived and pondered between two and three thousand years ago:

From delusion lead me to Truth.
From darkness lead me to Light.
From death lead me to Immortality.
(Brihad-aranyaka Upanishad 1.3.28 in Mascaro 1965: 127)

Second, as reported nearly two thousand years ago in Christian scripture:

Pilate said to him, 'So you are a king?' Jesus
answered, 'You say that I am a king. For this I was
born and for this I have come into the world, to bear
witness to the truth. Every one who is of the truth
hears my voice.' Pilate said to him, 'What is truth?'
(John 18.37-8)

Third, from Islam:

God is Al-Haqq – 'The Real', the supreme reality of
all existence, whose nearness, judgement, and will are
the great facts of human life.
(Cragg 1985: 35)

Fourth, from the Sikhs' first Guru, Guru Nanak (1469-1539):

One reality is, truth by name.
(Adi Granth I, see Singh 1995: I, 47)

Openness requires me to come clean about my autobiographical reasons for starting with these four quotations, especially as the invitation to be a Swarthmore lecturer is connected with one's individual life story. My concern with faith communities and traditions goes deeper than my current appointment as Senior Lecturer in Religions and Education in the University of Warwick's Institute of Education. I was brought up in an explicitly Christian household in the south of England. My family and almost all my family's friends were, as far as I know, English. But I was as a child intrigued by knowing that I had Scottish ancestors, and by hearing my one Jewish secondary school friend talk about 'shul' (synagogue) and about Middle Eastern politics. When, especially in the congregation of one church in the New Forest, I came across Romanies, my imagination and interest in their very different life experience was fired.

My reason for attending services in this church (an Italianate chapel belonging to the local aristocrat) was that, as a lay reader in the Church of England, my father accepted invitations to officiate in various rural churches. Later, while I was an undergraduate reading Classics, he was ordained, as a deacon and then to serve as one of the first Auxiliary Pastoral Ministers in the diocese of Winchester. His step came when my own responses to Christianity were in turmoil, and it precipitated me into academic study of theology. This was in 1970, the year that I first attended a Quaker Meeting for Worship – in Jesus Lane, Cambridge.

It was during my undergraduate years that two Christian priests, Kenneth Cragg and John Bowker, moved me by their personal engagement with Islam. Kenneth Cragg inspired me with the poetry of what he said. His *The Call of the Minaret* (2nd ed 1985) introduced me to Islam, and his compilation of Muslim and Christian prayer (1970) first set me thinking about the possibility of prayer transcending divides of faith allegiance. John Bowker's lectures spoke of an intense identification with a mediaeval Muslim master called Abu Hamid Muhammad al-Ghazzali (d.1111 CE). Al-Ghazzali was a 'formidable scholar' who 'underwent a crisis brought on by an awareness that although he was lecturing *about* God, he did not know God' (Bowker 1997: 44). Al-Ghazzali's brilliant career as professor in Baghdad ended in mental breakdown. After living as a Sufi he returned to academic debate, affirming the value not only of the rational sciences but also of personal experience (Robinson 1996). Through John Bowker's lectures al-Ghazzali lived anew in the 1970s in the Divinity School in Cambridge.

The only certainty that surfaced from my personal 'churning of the ocean' (to borrow not a Muslim but a Hindu image) was that I must head for India – which I did in 1974, after training as a teacher. For much of the past nearly 30 years I have worked as a teacher and as a fieldworker studying south Asian communities in Britain, especially young Hindus and Sikhs (Jackson and Nesbitt 1993; Nesbitt 2000). As an interpreter of Hindu and Sikh tradition, through my writing and lecturing, I have been living at an interface. Through marriage into a Punjabi Hindu family I cannot dodge the undertow, where communities merge. As an educationist, helping equip teachers to provide religious education in schools, my day to day challenge is how teachers can best enable pupils to learn both about world faiths and from them. A recent exercise (Nesbitt and Kaur 1999) aimed to bring to young readers the insights of Guru Nanak, the first of the Sikhs' ten Gurus. This focused my thinking on Guru Nanak's understanding of truth, and on how this connects with those of us who are not Sikhs.

Further, more recent context for what I am undertaking is best summarised by the date: September 11th. In September 2001 I was roughly halfway through a preliminary draft of this book when the attacks on the United States took place and President George W. Bush flung the words 'crusade' and 'evil' around the globe. Samuel P. Huntington's book, with its startling title, *The Clash of Civilizations* (1996), came to my notice. Its theme is that societies define themselves in conflict with each other, and that Islam and Christianity routinely do so. After September 11th we all realised that interfaith relations had an even more urgent topicality than in previous years, which had seen their own share of incidents of anti-semitism (see Runnymede Commission on Antisemitism 1997), Islamophobia (see Commission on British Muslims and Islamophobia 1997) and genocide. Efforts to increase non-Muslims' understanding of Muslims now have a special urgency, partly because more complex political relations can so easily be simplified down to Islam against the rest. More than ever before, people all over the world now know that they are caught up in a single web.

However, understanding Islam is not the particular emphasis of this book. In fact I shall – because of my own experience – be drawing rather more often on Hinduism and Sikhism than on Islam or other faith traditions. But my hope is that this book endorses ways of looking at things which open us to understanding Muslims as well as people of faith more generally.

As you can see, my opening selection of quotations about truth not only provides a context but it also has a particular context in my individual history. Similarly your favourite quotations and maxims belong uniquely in your history. At this point I invite you to scrutinise, ponder and acknowledge the multiple influences at work in your own life. Later chapters will make it clearer why, in approaching 'other faiths', it is helpful to interrogate ourselves and review our own stories of who we are. My own journey so far has brought me into contact with some of the traditions of India rather than of Africa, China, Japan or many other sources of insight. The absence of, for example, direct reference to Confucian teaching in this book reflects my incomplete experience – it is certainly not a value judgement.

Our religiously plural society

Society in the UK is repeatedly described as plural, often with the rider that this is a recent, challenging and less than ideal state of affairs, if only because of tensions that surface as periodic local unrest which captures the headlines. By a plural society we mean one that consists of individuals and groups – many in locally significant numbers – with family histories linked to different parts of the world, and with different religions and cultures. This is of course neither a local nor a new phenomenon, except insofar as every mix of individuals in every place and time is unique.

Centuries ago spiritual masters, the writers of spiritual texts and the Christian 'early church fathers', lived in religiously and culturally diverse societies. From the Bible we hear how close the patriarchs and prophets were to Egyptians, Assyrians, Babylonians, Philistines and worshippers of Baal. Jesus and Guru Nanak lived in territories (Palestine and Punjab) that were under an invader's occupation (Roman and Muslim respectively). Muhammad was born in Makkah when it was a major centre at the crossroads of trade routes. He probably met Jews and Christians as well as worshippers of local gods – the Qur'an certainly mentions a variety of groups.

This being so, we may look to what we know of the teaching and conduct of prophets and gurus in order to work out what their responses were, and whether these can serve us as models for spiritually enlightened engagement with 21st century plurality. The Hebrew prophets' denunciations of 'going after other gods', as interpreted by Europeans, have contributed to a European consciousness that has manifested itself not only in disciplined monotheism but also in hostility to non-Christian minorities. Clearly, if we are committed to fostering social harmony and greater respect and understanding between groups, in our reading of the Jewish scriptures which Christians know as the Old Testament, we do well to concentrate on exhortations to welcome the stranger (eg Deuteronomy 10.19). In the Christian gospels Jesus affirmed the faith of the Roman centurion (Luke 7.9) and told a story about a marginalised

Samaritan traveller in order to illustrate practical compassion (Luke 10.30-37). At the same time both Jesus and Guru Nanak opposed hypocrisy: and there are those who regard the liberal tolerance, with which many of us may be more comfortable, as just this – a form of hypocrisy – because it papers over issues. So we are left guessing what exactly Moses, Muhammad or Guru Nanak would have proclaimed to Bradford or Brixton or, indeed, to Britain Yearly Meeting, although we may have pretty clear ideas on the basis of our reading and our beliefs.

Plural societies are not a new phenomenon, but their scale is: never before have people from so many backgrounds lived at such close quarters. What is new is the global extent of cultural diversity plus the speed of migration and settlement and our awareness of this, thanks to the international media coverage. Speed characterises not only the way in which people travel, but the communication between them, telephoning, e-mailing and text-messaging each other across continents.

You will be familiar with terms that are used for this unprecedentedly fluid, globally interconnected society in which we live and for this period of human history: globalisation, the global village, late modernity and post-modernity spring to mind. Especially when discussing what 'post-modern' means, scholars emphasise the fact that people no longer accept and share the same framework or the same 'grand narrative' or way of making sense of everything. In fact there is increasing acceptance that there is no one account of how things are that is uniquely true. Certainly, in a society composed of Christians, Jews, Hindus and adherents to other faiths, different people will have different understandings of 'God', of human behaviour and of what happens to us after we die.

Secularisation and fundamentalism

But society does not simply consist of believers in different faiths, it may arguably be better understood as consisting of, on the one hand, 'faith-full' people and, on the other hand, 'secular' people. By 'secular' I mean, for example, those children – in many British schools the majority – who say 'I am nothing' when asked to name their religion (Rudge 1998). But, of course, it would be simplistic to divide society up in this way into two categories. Most of us are aware not of a sharp divide but of a spectrum from 'I am nothing', through nominal allegiance, to explicit – and in some cases all-consuming – commitment to a particular faith. We know from opinion polls that many more people claim to believe in God than actually attend places of worship. Moreover, 'being nothing' does not necessarily mean apathy to ethical issues or to social concerns, any more than 'being something' (Christian, Hindu etc), in the sense of claiming a religious label, means being any more concerned about these or indeed about spirituality.

Secularisation is the name given to one process that is under way in our religiously plural society. As people become more secular religion is no longer part of their personal or family identity (or at least it is no longer such an important aspect of how they describe themselves) (Voas 2003). What they 'believe' may contribute to poll statistics (depending on how the question is phrased), but their beliefs don't affect their lives.

A simultaneous development is the increase in fundamentalism of many sorts. Strictly speaking, 'fundamentalism' is usually a misnomer. Historically the term was used first for a Christian doctrine of the inerrancy of the Bible and, consistently with this, of beliefs such as creation in seven days and the virgin birth. In popular usage 'fundamentalism' is used for religious fanaticism often expressed in political militancy. Certainly we recognise the trend for more and more individuals to join groups which make exclusive religious and political claims, and which will in some cases use extreme – sometimes violent –

methods. Yet fundamental to a religion's teaching may be love and compassion, not hatred and anger. Fundamentalism (in terms of rigid belief and passionate aggression) is one response to plurality and to secularisation. All three need and feed each other (see eg Armstrong 2000).

Intrafaith diversity

Another aspect of our plural society is the diversity *within* its constituent communities of faith. As well as the continuum from secular to 'committed' and on to 'fundamentalist', this intrafaith diversity is the sum of differences of gender, generation, ethnicity and different levels of education and wealth. The diversity is denominational too. As far as Christians are concerned we are probably keenly aware of differences between Catholic and Protestant, between Baptist and Quaker or indeed between 'high' and 'low' Anglicans. Among Christian groups we know of differences which are usually cultural or doctrinal or both. For example, my Cypriot friends' Greek Orthodox worship differs from my Jamaican neighbour's Pentecostal worship in the language that is used, in the manner of worshipping and in its theological emphases. At the same time we can recognise evident connections between the two congregations' beliefs and practices – the Bible, the life of Jesus and belief in his resurrection and the continuing activity of the Holy Spirit, for example. Yet we may overlook the fact that Hindu, Muslim and other communities are also heterogeneous, as well as overlapping.

The heterogeneity includes ethnic, cultural and linguistic diversity. (Is my Hindu friend a Gujarati or a Bengali?) We may already be aware that the majority of Muslims are Sunni and that a substantial minority are Shia, and will find it useful to discover more about what this distinction means. The diversity also includes groups who regard their religious allegiance in a different way from how it is viewed by people whom we (the outsiders) perceive to be other members of the same faith community. For example, the devout Sikh in your local interfaith group may be a Namdhari – as such he or she is likely to be strongly committed to vegetarianism and peace-making (Weller 2001: 610-612). Yet, from another Sikh viewpoint, Namdharis are not Sikhs at all, because they revere a living human Guru in addition to the ten human Gurus and the Guru as scripture (see chapter three) revered by (other) Sikhs. Once we start to find out about these groupings we also become aware of the tensions and differing perceptions within what we had previously assumed to be more uniform faith communities. Our Quaker history of dissent, and the current ambivalence concerning whether or not Quakers are Christians, can help us to recognise and understand differences of this kind.

Our spiritually plural selves

In addition to society's many variegated faiths there is another important way in which our society is plural. To appreciate this we need to be looking inwards. Does something in you resonate with these words of Francis Clooney, an American Jesuit scholar of Hinduism, in a lecture in 2002? 'Look into your own heart and you find different impulses that don't fit into your own religious tradition'. Are you aware of yourself as in any way 'spiritually plural'? Is this, at any rate, how neighbours – perhaps 'Evangelical' neighbours – perceive you? Perhaps you do not see yourself as spiritually plural, but as (for example) a Christian who sees fit to investigate other faiths or at least to be neighbourly to people from different communities. But consider the influences that intersect uniquely in you, through the generations and across the planet. Is not each of us in some sense a constellation? And our own plural spirituality is inextricably caught up in the plural spirituality which similarly characterises individuals who would variously put 'Hindu', 'Sikh', 'atheist' or 'C of E' on their hospital forms.

It is a plurality which includes the increasing number of 'dual membership' Friends. This is often dual membership in terms of Christian ecumenism, so that we have Anglican Quakers/ Quaker Anglicans. John Punshon extended this when he reminded us in the 1990 Swarthmore Lecture that 'Most Friends have come into the Society from other places, with formative influences ranging from Catholic sacramentalism to secular humanism' (1990: 40). We must remember too Friends' dual membership across faith boundaries. The three Bs come to mind: Bahai, Brahma Kumari, Buddhist. Over the years I have met a number of attenders and members of the Society of Friends whose spiritual discipline and insights draw strongly on these traditions.

The Bahais follow a faith which started with Baha'u'llah in Iran in the 1860s. They recognise many Manifestations of God, including Buddha, Jesus and Muhammad, and they have no priesthood. Bahais emphasise the need for the unity of all peoples and religions. Their prioritisation of peace, education and economic development projects resonates with Friends' concerns.

Whereas the Bahai faith emerged in a Muslim context, the Brahma Kumaris' historical roots are in the Hindu tradition. Brahma Kumaris were established in India in 1937 and derive inspiration from Dada Lekhraj, a Sindhi diamond merchant who came to be known as Prajapita Brahma. The Brahma Kumaris run centres which provide classes in meditation (*raja yoga*), which many seekers have found beneficial, not least those whose search is for means of coping with stress. Distinctively, Brahma Kumaris emphasise celibacy, and the leadership is (unusually for religious organisations) female. With Quakers and Bahais, Brahma Kumaris share a strong commitment to peace.

Our Friend, Jim Pym, has set out the fruitful possibility of being both Buddhist and Quaker (eg 2000: 77-89). We probably know seekers who have derived strength and tranquillity from Buddhist teachers and groups, and who have come with this experience to the local Meeting. One researcher, Klaus Huber, distinguishes 'Quaker Buddhists' (those with strong roots in Buddhism) from 'semi-Buddhist Quakers' (people who have remained closer to British Quaker orthodoxy) (2001: 80). Either way, many Quakers acknowledge a special debt to Buddhism, as is evident from *The Friend* (eg Gunward 2002).

Apart from the three Bs, we are likely to have encountered Jewish Friends and attenders in our meetings, and I know two Quaker Muslims/Muslim Quakers. Probably we can all add to this list of friends and Friends whose religiosity, if not their declared allegiance, is dual (or indeed multiple). We may ourselves, like a growing number of people, have experienced 'conversion', a transformation and a shift of allegiance from one faith to another. But as converts we do not leave behind all that we were before. St Paul did not forget the Jewish law!

Another aspect of our widespread plural spirituality is that we may have drawn spiritual nourishment from the ideas of a philosopher, a novelist or a psychotherapist. Indeed our most powerful conditioning may not be 'religious'. Yet the impact of religious messages may be clearer to us than the extent to which our reactions and priorities are affected and created by other pervasive assumptions – assumptions about normality, success and entitlement, which we do not regard as 'religious'. For example, at the time of writing this book, young people from many backgrounds – in the English speaking west at least – aspire to be 'cool', not 'sad'. To be cool means affecting a detached, slightly cynical stance – and having the right trainers and mobile phone. (A sad person lacks such attributes.) Permeating conversation, advertising, entertainment and journalism the values which most strongly influence us link us across our apparently different 'faiths'. This is the case whether or not, individually, we consciously accept or repudiate them. Recognising influences that connect us will help us when we come to look at ways in which more exclusive and more inclusive understandings of truth are related to each other. It will also help us to recognise the spiritual plurality of those whose perception of themselves is, however, more unitary and clearcut as straightforwardly Muslim or Christian believers.

Individuals' spirituality and religious practice – and certainly their family's – may be plural as a result of 'mixed marriage'. (And isn't every union in some sense mixed?) One researcher, Voas, has examined mixed marriages as an index (a cause or a result, or both) of the secularisation that I summarised above (2003). But my own experience suggests that far from necessarily weakening individuals' faith, marriage to someone of a different faith can serve as a test bed for spiritual growth. Partners may engage in soul-searching discussion (real interfaith dialogue) about what is negotiable, and what is not, in bringing up their children. But what I am calling plural spirituality is by no means peculiar to (or necessarily particularly marked in) members of mixed faith families.

In the Hindu context, in which some devotees readily include pictures of Jesus and Mary with Hindu deities in their shrines, people do not generally perceive a problem in acknowledging multiple gurus and sources of inspiration, or affirming the validity of all faiths. But in a Christian (or post-Christian) environment such an inclusive spirituality is too easily branded as 'New Age' or condemned as shallow or unsound.

Certainly there are circumstances in Britain at least in which only the naïve or the courageous acknowledge their plurality. Both 'syncretism' (putting together different beliefs) and 'eclecticism' (picking from a range of sources) are dirty words. In the wake of the 1988 Education Reform Act, following political and journalistic debate on the statutory requirement for 'multifaith RE', John Hull, Professor of Religious Education in the University of Birmingham, published a rigorous examination of the abundance of disparaging food metaphors that were being thrown around. He called his book *Mishmash* (1991). We have seen how, almost a decade later, when the then England football coach, Glenn Hoddle, confessed to belief in reincarnation, even responsible journalists' commentary was replete with intentionally derogatory images of a 'pastiche spirituality' and a religious 'supermarket', 'buffet', 'cafeteria' or 'smorgasbord'.

As we know, so called New Age writings and groups are lampooned for eclecticism. Here is one of the mildest expressions of concern – from a senior religious educationist:

> Even the religious skip in and out of one another's systems picking up bits to their liking. I may use Buddhist meditation techniques, a Hindu mantra, the Sermon on the Mount, the Ten Commandments and the *Avesta*, but commit myself to none of their originating religious bases. Is this ecumenism on the world's religious scene, or is it the Self risen to greater heights? (Copley 1998)

To take an example from the press – on 'what Canterbury needs in its 104th incumbent':

> It means embracing variety and diversity, without surrendering to a pick-and-mix spirituality, that wants only the benefits of religion without any of its duties and responsibilities. (Vallely 2002)

Both writers connect religious openness with selfishness. Choice, they suggest, is self-indulgent. But isn't choice inevitable? And, even if it is optional, it is not always a soft option. A Buddhist master's words are translated as 'The perfect way is difficult only for those who pick and choose' (Master Seng-T'san quoted in St.Ruth 1997: 14). His words too convey a sense that choosing is somehow perverse. But deciding that a way is the perfect way can also be experienced as (or appear to others as) a choice. The critics disapprove of a choice that mixes ideas from different sources and which fights shy of whole packages. But why is this inherently less commendable than accepting a single whole package?

We need to address the issue of choice and a religious supermarket the more seriously if John Punshon is right in identifying 'supermarket Quakerism' (1990: 23) such that 'the activist may have one shopping list, the contemplative another'. As he points out, this is in stark contrast to the 17th century, when becoming a Friend meant that 'you accepted the Truth as a whole and took the consequences'.

But can we not take heart from Damaris Parker-Rhodes' 1977 Swarthmore Lecture in which she made no bones about the fact that:

> A number of Friends both here and in America, are at the present time in this movement of search, practising Transcendental Meditation [TM], learning Yoga and T'ai Chi, Zen and Theravada Meditation and working with Sufis – and I count myself among them. This is not just shopping around, but is rather a serious experiment with truth which for me has made Quaker Christianity the more precious.
> (Parker-Rhodes 1977 in Pym 2000: 39)

Affirming our own spiritual plurality

The reality is that religiously serious people have since time immemorial exercised choice. From the start Christian theologians have thought and written in conscious relation to other beliefs and interpretations, often with a strong motivation to preserve what they saw as pure doctrine from corruption, from contamination with 'heathen' practice and outlook. My emphasis by contrast will be on celebrating a discerning, persevering eclecticism as a basis for religious revelation and insights in a spiritually rich world, as well as for coping with distress in a complex and challenging environment. This is an eclecticism which makes discernment and perseverance more, not less, important.

Faced as we are with such evident religious diversity the image of a discriminating collector springs to mind. I recall, in the early 1970s, an evening seminar given by Professor Charlie Moule on 'the personal canon'. He pointed out to us that Christians, whether 'fundamentalist' or more 'liberal', operate with selective canons of scripture, which consist of those passages which speak compellingly to them, consoling or challenging them. I noted at the time that my own canon had not only selected from the Bible, but also incorporated passages of Plato (Socrates speaking about death in the *Apology*), and verses of poets (Wordsworth's from 'Intimations of Immortality' and Francis Thompson's 'The Hound of Heaven'). How could it be otherwise?

But the plural spirituality that I am describing is not just a matter of creating an anthology. It requires a commitment to being open. In an editorial in 1999 Harry Albright, editor of *The Friend*, gave expression to this openness, and firmly connected it to Quaker understanding of the 'Light':

> For me it comes down to one of the central cores of my belief. If I am to accept, as I do, that we all have access to the Light, then it is only by joining together the bits of light that are given to me with those which are given to others that I can begin to see the whole... [I]t is always a question of give and take. And, as we are open to the giving, so we should be open to the

taking, even if, at the time, we fail to see the relevance
...of what we are being shown...We may accept, we
may reject, but to do either, we have to be open.
(1999: 2)

Of course being open and selecting a canon are fraught with
hazard. It is the Greek for taking or choosing which gives us
the emotive word 'heresy'. In early Christian history people
whose canons ranged wider than the canonical scripture (such
as Valentinus and other Gnostics) and those whose canon was
narrower (such as Marcion who excluded everything except
edited writing by Paul and Luke) were condemned as heretics
– as threats to the true faith and so worthy of death (Chidester
2000). Moreover the canons of individuals and groups can
mirror and strengthen unloving prejudice, rather than love. In
the twentieth century a focus on those biblical texts that
emphasised separation underpinned the apartheid that divided
South Africans, oppressing the majority (Chidester 2000).

In any case, more apposite than the images of collecting and
selecting is that of travelling, of being on a spiritual journey, of
being on the move rather than of hoarding. One example of
this comes from our Leeds Friend, Kim Knott. In an interview
Kim traced her path from a religionless childhood to her membership of the Religious Society of Friends (Nesbitt 1999a).
In her journey a key influence had been, she explained, her
study of the Hindu tradition, involving as it did both reading
religious material and conducting fieldwork among local
Hindus. In the course of this study Kim had felt drawn towards
bhakti, the Indian tradition of loving devotion to a personal
God. As a scholar she had subsequently explored ISKCON
(The International Society for Krishna Consciousness, also
known as Hare Krishna). It was, she acknowledged, ISKCON
devotees' exacting and transformative commitment which

impelled her to commit herself to a religious community (in her case the Quakers). So Kim's story is in fact one of becoming, rather than of travelling – let alone of simply collecting. So too with our own stories.

Travelling and becoming bring us to pilgrimage – and to the next chapter.

CHAPTER TWO

Interfaith Pilgrims

Thanne longen folk to goon on pilgrimages.
(Geoffrey Chaucer *The Canterbury Tales*, The General Prologue 1.9)

Pilgrims

Pilgrims: what does this word bring to mind? An expedition to Glastonbury or Iona? Or with Friends to 'George Fox country'? The motley, earthy characters of Geoffrey Chaucer's *Canterbury Tales*, making their boisterous 14th century way to the shrine of St Thomas à Becket at Canterbury? The frequently side-tracked pilgrim, Christian, whose progress John Bunyan charted three centuries later, weighed down by his burden and fleeing the City of Destruction?

Sunday matins and weekday morning assemblies in school spring to my mind, when I belted out the adaptation of Bunyan's poem:

He who would valiant be...
Let him in constancy
Follow the Master.

Certainly these words left me with an abiding sense of the ideal pilgrim's undeflected perseverance despite temptations. In less Protestant mode we may be thinking of travellers to Lourdes or Walsingham. Modern pilgrims often head for places where miracles are reported to occur – whether those of the South Indian 'incarnation', Sathya Sai Baba, or of the Virgin Mary.

Our growing awareness of what pilgrimage means to Hindus and Muslims can give 'pilgrim' fresh meaning for us. Imagine yourself joining the several million white-clad Muslim pilgrims who annually converge during the month of Hajj – the month of pilgrimage – on the city of Makkah in Saudi Arabia. Differences of wealth, education and ethnicity disappear in a sense of unity and solidarity, as the millions put on special plain clothes. For men these consist of two unstitched lengths of white cloth, one tied round the waist and reaching to their ankles, the other worn over the shoulders. Differences are irrelevant as all unite in prayer facing towards the *kaba*. This is the black cube at Islam's physical heart, the first house of God which was built by the prophet Adam.

Until the ceremonies of the month of Hajj are over, the pilgrim accepts a discipline. This means not putting on other clothes, not wearing shoes or cutting one's nails or hair. Nor may the pilgrim engage in sexual relations, take part in an argument, fight or hunt (Bowker 1997: 402). The pilgrimage includes walking around the *kaba* anticlockwise seven times as well as other actions at particular places with historic associations with Adam, Hawwa' (Eve), Ibrahim (Abraham), Isma'il (Ishmael) and Hagar. The 10th day is Id al Adha (also written in our roman script as Eid-ul-Adha), the festival of sacrifice, which recalls Ibrahim's sacrifice. The pilgrims sacrifice an animal to eat and give part of the meat to the needy. *Hajjis* return home, uplifted and transformed by the blessing which they have shared. But there will be some pilgrims who are prevented from setting out to Makkah, or who never arrive. Allah will bless and forgive them no less than those who completed the course – for what counts in the eyes of Allah is one's intention (*niyyah*).

Can we look too at what Hindus mean by pilgrimage? As one entry point I recommend our Friend Geoffrey Maw's sensitive narrative of his encounters at the river Narmada's holy sites and in the mountains of north India in the 1920s and 1930s (Maw no date and 1997; Dart 1995: 79-83). For Hindus a pilgrimage is a journey to a hallowed place, a threshold between human and divine. For this threshold the word is *tirth*, literally a ford across a river. Many such 'fords' are shrines situated beside a river (especially at a confluence) or by the sea. Like Jerusalem, Rome or Makkah, these 'fords' draw pilgrims thousands of miles. Especially at astrologically determined auspicious times, Hindu pilgrims arrive – in their millions in the case of the 12 yearly Kumbh Mela at the sacred confluence on which the north Indian city of Allahabad is situated. Such a place is, at the very least in metaphorical terms, the crossing point from the cycles of birth, death and rebirth to the release from endlessly being born and reborn.

Another aspect of Hindu pilgrimage may be less apparent to us. A colleague in Leicester was preparing a largely Hindu class for their General Certificate of Secondary Education examination in religious education. She showed them a 'model answer' on 'why Hindus go on pilgrimages'. This included the significance of journeys and sacred space, but from their own experience her pupils knew that going on pilgrimage was usually to do with a relative fulfilling an obligation – usually the duty of taking a deceased parent's ashes to immerse in a holy river in India. Or it might be a vow to perform a particular rite at a particular temple. Pilgrimage might arise out of obligation but was then experienced as bringing transformation.

Our own reflection on Hindu and Muslim pilgrimage may find a different focus which deepens our understanding. As an artist, our Friend Adam Boulter has reflected in this cross-cultural way on 'spirituality in the wilderness' more than most, while preparing to paint in St Hugh's Charterhouse, Borough, Southwark. His five paintings are inspired by five faiths. On the theme of one painting, the Hindu walking pilgrimage through the Himalayas, he writes:

> Relating to God is not an achievement…We don't achieve it at the end of a Pilgrimage; God walks with us the whole way. (Boulter no date: 75)

Some words of George Fox come to mind: 'There are too many talkers, and few walkers in Christ' (Epistle 353 in Ambler 2001: 82).

Although Sikhs, too, have a high regard for places of popular pilgrimage, the Sikh scriptures convey Guru Nanak's insight that the true 'ford', the actual point of crossing from earth to heaven, is the Nam (God's name, which is also Truth). In other words, it is when we focus all our attention contemplatively on continuous inner remembrance of what truly is that we are truly pilgrims.

So, in deciding on the word pilgrim for the title of this book I was identifying our quest for truth as a spiritual journey – one which transcends human cultures. It is a journey in which we have to leave most of our baggage behind. And it may require a discipline. It is an adventure in which we have companions, literally alongside us as well as centuries and generations before us. There may be maps and anecdotes to exchange, but there will be times too when the journey feels dauntingly or excitingly 'uncharted' – to quote my late friend Roger Hooker, a pioneering interfaith explorer (1973).

In drawing attention to the resonance of 'pilgrim' over centuries and across communities I am modelling a method. By taking time to reflect on familiar terms (such as pilgrim) in a historical perspective and in a cross-cultural, interfaith way, we can experience it more fully and spark insights into the fullness of truth for which we are headed. For example, the Muslim emphasis on the prime importance of intention (rather than on completion) may encourage us when adversity intervenes.

We have considered pilgrimage in an interfaith way. In the rest of this chapter, as we equip ourselves for pilgrimage, we look at the meaning of two key terms – 'interfaith' and 'faith' – and, through two stories, I shall be affirming the pilgrim's need not only to travel but, while doing so, to encounter the 'other'.

Interfaith

Some people avoid writing 'interfaith' as a single, unhyphenated word 'for fear of giving the impression of a movement that blurs the distinctiveness of the religious traditions involved' (Weller 2001: 80). The word 'interfaith' made it, unhyphenated, into the *New Oxford Dictionary of English* in 1998, but what we would now call interfaith initiatives have a much longer history. There is a tendency in the west to think in terms of Christian initiatives and to see 1893 as a seminal date, as it was in this year that the first Parliament of the World's Religions was hosted in Chicago. I like to go back earlier to mention the Mughal Emperor of India, Akbar the Great (1542-1605 CE). Akbar regarded himself as a Muslim, but proclaimed a new religion which drew on several faiths. In his 'house of worship' in Fatehpursikri, near Agra, leaders of different faiths – including Jesuits – met together for discussion.

Encounters between members of different faiths certainly predate Akbar by well over 2000 years. But most encounters have had (and in many cases continue to have) agendas which are far from 'interfaith' in our present sense which communicates an *intention of understanding*. This is because domination and conversion, rather than listening and learning, have often been guiding principles. This has been especially true of Christians' and Muslims' encounters with 'other faiths', as well as with 'unsound' variants of their own faith.

The 20th century saw two key developments in promoting understanding between groups: the ecumenical movement brought together members of different Christian denominations, and interfaith initiatives have brought together people of different faiths at local, national and international level. The World Congress of Faiths was founded in 1936 to link individuals from different faiths. Since then 'interfaith' has become almost synonymous with 'dialogue', and a major purpose of encounter has been to increase mutual understanding and respect through conversation.

Within Britain Yearly Meeting the responsibilities of QCCIR, the Quaker Committee for Christian and Interfaith Relations, include 'keeping Britain Yearly Meeting informed of...opportunities for interfaith dialogue' (*Quaker faith & practice* 9.13). Of recent years many Friends have been active in fostering and encouraging interfaith awareness and activities both locally and nationally. I recall that in 1993 Woodbrooke together with the then 'CCR Interfaith Sub-Committee' held a conference on 'developing interfaith understanding'. Participants drew on ideas set out by Rex Ambler, Adam Curle, Martyn Grubb, Tom Gulliver, John Hall, Chris Lawson, Marion McNaughton, Margot Tennyson, Swami Tripurananda and myself. In 1997 Rex Ambler, Hugh Pyper and I were invited to contribute to a study day entitled 'Towards a Theology of Interfaith', organised by QCCIR (now better known as CIR).

Beyond our Society, interfaith dialogue has challenged the accepted beliefs of many Christians. For how can the moral imperative of loving, respecting and understanding one's neighbour be reconciled with the 'great commission' and the need to save souls? The 'great commission' is the name given to Jesus' words, after the resurrection, as reported in Matthew 28.18-20. These words begin:

All authority in heaven and earth has been given to me. Go therefore and make disciples of all nations, baptizing them in the name of the Father and of the Son and of the Holy Spirit...

Alan Race has clarified three broad Christian approaches to the 'theology of religions' (or ways of understanding how the belief systems of religions relate to each other). He is not 'pre-scribing' these approaches (Williams 2000: 95) but rather identifying the three possible perspectives which Christians in fact adopt as 'exclusivist', 'inclusivist' and 'pluralist', each of which comes in many varieties (2001). In a nutshell (and without doing justice to any of the three) the exclusivist believes that 'outside the church there is no salvation', no authentic revelation. Inclusivists hold the view that Christ (the universal saviour) is at work in faiths other than Chris-tianity, and so these faiths can be vehicles of salvation, but it is salvation in Christian terms. Pluralists affirm different faiths as valid in their own way, rather than trying to fit them into a Christian, Hindu or other faith-specific schema.

It is likely that for many Quakers reaching a sympathetic understanding of our exclusivist Christian neighbours is more challenging than entering into the thought world of adherents to other faiths.

If, as an interfaith pilgrim, you wish to inform yourself of the possibilities and pitfalls of reaching a theology of religions there is nowhere better to start than Alan Race's wise and authoritative book *Interfaith Encounter: The Twin Tracks of Theology and Dialogue* (2001). His chapter five, 'Track Two: The Dia-logue Loop', will introduce you to the literature on interfaith dialogue, and usefully distinguishes the spirit of dialogue in actual practice from the theological frameworks for it. The journal which Alan Race co-edits, *Interreligious Insight: a journal of dialogue and engagement* (which in 2003 takes over from *World Faiths Encounter*), will also keep you in touch with the ideas, concerns and practical projects of interfaith pilgrims and organisations from many backgrounds.

Especially if you are a teacher you may be interested in the potential for involving children and young people in dialogue. If so I commend the innovative approach of Julia Ipgrave (2001). Julia Ipgrave teaches in a primary school in which most pupils are from Indian Muslim families. She realised that the non-Muslim children's religious understanding was developing through dialogue with their Muslim peers – in fact they were engaged in active theology. She has worked imaginatively to facilitate this process and has developed guidance for teachers. For example she shows ways in which children can be equipped with the language necessary for articulating agreement, disagreement and enquiry. She provides examples of activities, including dialogue by e-mail between pupils at schools which are, in terms of the families' religious backgrounds, very different.

Interfaith encounter has an ethical as well as a theological dimension, and this can be summed up in the initiative to agree, declare and implement 'a global ethic'. (For more details, references and discussion see Race 2001: 124-143.) As we shall be pondering, in chapter five of this book, there are indeed convergences between faiths, and ethics is an obvious area of convergence. The values of compassion, peace and justice are often cited as exemplifying common ground. Since 11 September 2001 a new urgency has resounded in the calls by people of faith for shared values to be publicly affirmed and brought to bear. This is imperative for survival. For example:

It is urgent, therefore, that people of faith having come together to understand each other now seek a dialogue with political, economic and business leaders so that the moral values which are shared by the great religions become the basis for a just and peaceful world order. (Braybrooke 2002: 3)

Apart from theology and ethics, a further dimension of interfaith initiatives continues to find expression in interreligious worship and interfaith prayer. This arises in many forms and arouses particularly emotional discussion. To this we will return in chapter four.

You may be thinking, 'These few comments on interfaith are all very well, if rather abstract, but I just want some practical help on how best to get started. I don't have any Hindu, Buddhist or Muslim friends and I don't know where to begin.' This is where the Inter Faith Network for the United Kingdom and another publication, *Religions in the UK* (Weller 2001), can help!

The Inter Faith Network for the United Kingdom was set up in 1987 and makes communication easier between a wide range of faith-based organisations. For example its one-page code entitled 'Building Good Relations with People of Different Faiths and Beliefs' provides a sensitively constructive basis for whatever we decide to do – whether organising a meeting, visiting an unfamiliar place of worship or initiating a conversation that goes deeper than passing pleasantries.

Together with the University of Derby, the Network has produced the third edition of its multifaith directory (Weller 2001). For all of us with concerns for building bridges between faith-related communities this is an invaluable resource which should be in all public libraries. The directory lists places of worship and organisations for each of the faith communities –

alphabetically, from Bahai to Zoroastrian – and it sets out detailed guidance for anyone wishing to make contact with members of faith communities, to visit unfamiliar places of worship, and to avoid behaving insensitively.

Do not hesitate to contact CIR (see above) via Friends House. This Committee now has a commission to Yearly Meeting to engage with local Meetings in considering the issues involved in making local contacts, and two national conferences have been held at Friends House to encourage Friends' local interfaith activity. Keep a lookout for organised interfaith initiatives, including any at Woodbrooke. At the same time let us remember the fluid plurality of our social and spiritual existence and reflect critically on the word 'interfaith'.

Dimensions of faith

'Interfaith' suggests that there is our faith (Christianity? Quakerism?) on the one hand and that there are other faiths in contradistinction to this. If I had entitled this book 'Quakers and Other Faiths' or even 'Quakers and People of Other Faiths' it would fall into a trap and reinforce some of the assumptions that I am challenging. There are two problems – one with the word 'other', the second with the word 'faith', or for that matter 'religion'. It is with 'faith' that I will start.

The English word 'faith' denotes a quality (confidence, firm belief) and has also become a synonym for organised religion. So we can speak of the Hindu faith, the Sikh faith and so on. In my own professional field of religious education 'faith', 'faith tradition' and 'tradition' are currently more acceptable than 'religion' for this purpose.

Religious studies provide tools for unravelling what 'faith' and 'religion' mean. One of these is the idea of faiths having many dimensions. Ninian Smart, an influential scholar in this field, suggested examining each religion in terms of six – and later seven – 'dimensions'. These dimensions he called the practical and ritual; the experiential and emotional; the narrative and mythical; the doctrinal and philosophical; the ethical and legal; the social and institutional; and the material or aesthetic dimension. This last dimension included the art, architecture and sacred places of each religion (Smart 1989: 12-21). We might come up with our own different list of 'dimensions', and it can be a useful exercise to 'unpack' in this way what religion means to us.

Whatever list we adopt, we may begin to note a Quaker tendency to select one or two dimensions of another tradition to compare with Quakerism. For example, Friends have made connections between Quakerism and mystically oriented texts (see, for instance, Dart 1989). In the case of the Hindu tradition this means that Friends have dwelt appreciatively on verses in the Upanishads, rather than on the complexities of the caste system or on the wealth of images of gods and goddesses. But do we always recognise the extent to which we are selecting particular 'dimensions'?

To take another example: Quakers may make links between the Quaker emphasis on nonviolence and nonviolent activists, in particular Mohandas Karamchand (Mahatma) Gandhi. *Ahimsa* (nonviolence), as espoused and demonstrated by Gandhi, is a recurrent theme. This tendency means that it is all too easy for us to overlook other strong elements of Hindu tradition and society, namely the apparent affirmation or legitimation of war (as a last resort at least) provided by the two great epics, the Mahabharata and the Ramayana, and the undisputed place of the Kshatriya (traditionally warrior) class in Hindu society.

This selectivity may be partly because our instinct is to affirm others and to avoid criticising their tradition. Indeed courtesy and sensitivity require this – but we must be aware of what we are doing. The resultant insights are often inspirational and reassuring, but we need to supplement them with more multi-dimensional approaches if we are to engage in a more realistic and grounded way with people – rather than with books, ideas, pigeon-holes and labels. As interfaith pilgrims we may surprise ourselves by finding inspiration in dimensions, such as ritual, which we had previously played down.

In what follows I hope to affirm some more dimensions of 'other faiths'. Community, identity, history, culture, values, concepts, ritual and iconography (pictures and three dimensional images) are dimensions that would repay our efforts to explore. Of course these can be separated out from each other only in abstract discussion. In practice there are no divides between them. Worship (a warmer word than ritual) will be the dimension that we begin to open up in this book (in chapter four) as we approach other faiths.

I have included community, identity, history and culture as dimensions of religion. But we could just as well regard religion as one strand in all these. What matters to us as interfaith pilgrims is that we understand the potency of all these, and the fact that for our neighbour these may be far more powerful aspects of being a Muslim, Hindu etc than any of the 'truths' that we identify in holy books or in accounts of the faith concerned. As interfaith pilgrims we are likely to feel more challenged by assumptions about family authority, and by the expectations of and by women, or by interpretations of contested history (in Cyprus, Kashmir, Israel – the list is long) than we are by the statements about God or the afterlife that we tend to place centre stage in our conceptions of a 'faith'.

Other

We have teased out some of the meaning of 'faith', but what about the word 'other'? Talking of people as other is a thread through everyone's experience. From our earliest childhood we learn how to distinguish one sort of person (baby, man, white, brown-eyed, clever, nasty) from another sort (teenager, woman, black, blue-eyed, stupid, nice). Social psychologists explain that grouping others in different categories is part of the process whereby we construct our own sense of individual and group identity.

Famously, the American Arab scholar, Edward Said, has drawn attention to the ways in which writers from western, colonising societies have treated – or rather created – the exotic other, for example in their representation of Islam, and how they have continuously defined the Oriental in their own terms (Said 1985). By naming and defining they have exercised power. They have determined how 'others' are conceived of in politically, economically and intellectually more influential societies, and in the process they have deeply affected how members of less powerful societies apprehend themselves.

To give an example of this tendency, Hindus (the people of India) spoke (long before Westerners introduced the word 'Hinduism' in the 19th century anyway), of their *dharma*. This was the behaviour expected of them in accordance with individuals' gender, relative seniority and birthright status in the hierarchy of *varna* (translated often as caste). Thus an unmarried daughter's *dharma* was different from her married sister's. A businessman's would differ from a priest's, and a young person's from an octogenarian's. A thirty-year-old man's *dharma* was to be a husband, a father, a householder working to support his family. On the other hand the dharma of a grandfather would be to concentrate more and more on spiritual pursuits in preparation for the final surrender of leaving this life. Clearly religion, *dharma* and Hinduism have different connotations. But it is *dharma*, or *sanatana dharma* – ancient, unchanging *dharma* – that is translated into English as Hinduism. Much recent scholarship, in anthropology for example, has been concerned to get beyond and behind the lenses and influence of European concepts and imperial domination.

Stories can, more effectively than scholarship, unsettle our assumptions – in this case about 'others' and 'people of other faiths'. But we are so familiar with some stories that fresh insights dawn only slowly. Here are two stories of Jewish travellers' encounters with the other, with someone of an (at least to some extent) different faith:

In the first of these stories – which the rabbi, Jesus, narrated to his entourage – a Jew was travelling from Jerusalem to Jericho (Luke 10.30-37). On the way the traveller was mugged. As he lay by the side of the road two leading members of his religious community caught sight of him, then hurried on without stopping. The third person to come along was a Samaritan, someone from a minority that Jews tended to condemn for their unorthodoxy and lack of purity. Their Israelite ancestors had, it was rumoured, married non-Jews 700 years before. Predictably, with hindsight, this man on the margins was the person who came to the victim's rescue, attending to his needs with imaginative and practical compassion.

Hasidic Jews tell the tale of a more recent rabbi, Eisik, son of Yekel, who lived in a ghetto in Cracow, and dreamed that he was commanded to go to Prague where he would find a great treasure that had been hidden under the bridge leading to the castle of the king of Bohemia. Obediently Rabbi Eisik travelled to Prague and waited by the bridge for many days. Then one night the Christian captain of the guard of the bridge asked him why he was there. When he heard about the rabbi's dream the captain roared with laughter – he had himself been instructed in a dream to set off for Cracow and search for a treasure that had been buried in a dirty corner behind the stove of a Jewish rabbi called Eisik son of Yekel. This, said the captain, was ridiculous as everyone in the ghetto was either called Eisik or

Yekel. Hearing this the rabbi said nothing but set off home, and there, behind the stove, he unearthed the treasure (Zimmer 1946; Doniger O'Flaherty 1999).

Each of these stories involves a traveller's transforming encounter with a stranger from another religious community. In the first case the Samaritan deliberately, and at personal cost, provided for the unfortunate Jewish wayfarer. In the second case the Christian captain was unaware of the beneficial impact of his dismissive words. In their different ways the stranger/neighbour served as healer and signpost. I use the word 'neighbour' deliberately throughout this book with just these qualities in mind.

The backdrop to both these transforming events is the human drive to stereotype – the inferior Samaritan, the dirty inhabitants of the ghetto with only two names between them. Both narratives depend on their listeners reading human society in 'us and them' terms of ourselves and the others.

The idiom of 'other faiths' (apparently value neutral at first glance) defines fellow humans in often overly rigid categories, and it distances them from us. This too is a form of stereotyping. It is a short step from Hindu to Hinduism, from Muslim to Islam, and our very desire to learn more locks people into religion-labelled boxes, and so into ghettos in our minds. If we are intelligent, well-meaning citizens we may be trying to learn more about the box and its label and not even notice whether our neighbour fits into it only with difficulty or only from certain angles. We too easily forget the individual plurality that I have emphasised.

Here it is very helpful to recall occasions when we have been the subjects of stereotype, often with no ill will intended. Many Friends – especially those who have lived overseas – will have had experiences like mine in the 1970s in India. I remember the jolting absurdity of realising that I was seen by many as part of a homogeneous lump – as white and so, necessarily, English, Christian, and meat-eating. I was classified in some local conversation as either a hippy or a missionary. (Whether these two were perceived as synonyms or a contrasting pair was not always clear.) Later I was to learn further from the experience of Indian friends (who were acquainted with Britain) assuming that as a westerner I would have no feeling for parents or older relatives. Westerners don't. (The fact that so many people sent their parents off to institutions, to old people's homes, rather than lovingly caring for them at home was evidence for this.) On another occasion I heard one of my colleagues (who had worked in London) explaining that English people couldn't work from first principles or improvise because they were too used to mod cons and to having written instructions like recipes and knitting patterns to follow.

As long as we stereotype our neighbours we may be less open to the healing and guidance which they have to offer us. We need the other in order to 'meet the other "in and as myself"' (Race 2001: 88 quoting Panikkar 1978: 40). It is the other who helps us to find our own purchase on truth. With this realisation the German scholar Heinrich Zimmer reflected on the story of Eisik son of Yekel in these words:

> Now the real treasure…is never far away…But there
> is the odd and persistent fact…that the one who
> reveals to us the meaning of our cryptic inner
> message must be a stranger, of another creed and a
> foreign race. (1946: 219-221)

To go further, it is the 'other' who may disclose to us the 'Other' (in the sense of God, Spirit, Truth). In the words of the educationist Dwayne Huebner: 'our relationship with and indebtedness to that "Other" [is] often manifested through the neighbour and the strange' (1993: 23). By welcoming the stranger we may be, in biblical language, welcoming an angel unawares. 'The practice of hospitality…speaks of God in our midst' (Barnes 2000: 12).

Reflexivity

And in encounters we are changed. This has been brought home to me in my experience of what is technically called the ethnographic study of religious communities. This experience has meant devoting years to fieldwork, consisting of listening (to what people tell me in interviews for instance) and observing (with varying degrees of participation on my part) in community events, celebrations, children's classes and so forth. Over the years I have realised more and more keenly the ways in which the researcher and the 'field' (the other) change each other. From the researcher's first steps toward formulating a research question through to the final editorial decisions on quoting interviewees and portraying their community in a report the researcher is a catalyst. In turn the researcher may, like Kim Knott in the previous chapter, be aware of being changed. This is not only the case with encounters that occur during research. The South African Muslim activist, Farid Esack, has written:

> The self cannot walk away from any meaningful
> encounter with the Other without carrying some of
> that Otherness along, and leaving some of the Self
> behind. (1997: 15)

In chapter three I shall be giving examples of the sorts of 'lenses' that we pilgrims all look through, because of growing up in particular cultures and speaking the language that we do. A reflexive approach will help us to think carefully about how our own faith allegiance or stance connects us with the experience of the person whom we are approaching. To what extent are we outsiders or insiders to their experience? For instance, the fact that we both profess a religious faith or are concerned with spirituality means that we already inhabit a similar terrain. It is possible that our openness links participants from different communities of faith with a strength of shared outlook which sets us apart from many of our respective co-religionists. Reflexivity leads us to ask if 'interfaith' itself is, indeed, a membership group determined by shared values, concerns and aspirations.

A member of an interfaith group in the diocese of Oxford has shared this reflection – and it sets the scene for chapter three:

> Even what I call 'interfaith' encounters are really personal encounters involving a spectrum of difference, shading from nationality through ethnicity, language, religious belief and religious practice to other broadly cultural facets. And why stop there?
>
> Everything about me and everything about the other are part of the meeting or partial meeting which takes place between us.
> (Anne Bowker no date: 26)

CHAPTER THREE

Using each other's lenses

What other judgement can I judge by but my own?
(Bernard Shaw: *St Joan* scene 6)

Treating my neighbour as myself

'Do to others what you would have done to yourself' is the Golden Rule which runs across religious traditions – as our Friend Margot Tennyson, in her text for an interfaith millennium event, reminded us (1998: 53-55). Jewish readers will recall Rabbi Hillel's response to Shammai's challenge to teach him the whole Torah while standing on one foot: Hillel replied, 'What is hateful to you, do not do to your neighbour: that is the whole Torah: all the rest of it is commentary; go and learn.' (Talmud, Shabbat 31a in Tennyson 1998: 55).

But as I have talked and listened, and moved from one person's sacred space to another's, I have realised the need to educate my readiness to treat everyone in the same way. Loving my neighbour as myself requires the effort to listen carefully for different assumptions, sensitivities and priorities from those which I too easily assume are common to us all, or are 'common sense'.

Lens is the metaphor with which I start this chapter, because our experience of perceiving things differently as a result of the glasses that we wear is an appropriate starting point for what is to follow. We shall look at a few instances of different perception in a literally visual sense. Then, picking up a thread from chapter two – the need to be reflexive, to develop an awareness of how we affect what we are looking at and reporting – we examine our own lenses. I will suggest that, for example, we look carefully at what we take for granted as Quakers.

From examination of our own lenses we will move on to looking at the world through a few other lenses. To do this I suggest considering that, in the area of 'religion', our neighbour may have different priorities and be asking different questions from ours. Also, translations into other languages can set us looking at what is familiar 'with new eyes'. From the many concepts that I could have chosen I have decided on one from Indian religious tradition – a concept which I initially render in English as 'polishing'.

My hope is that, if we proceed in this manner, not only will others appreciate our receptivity, but we will learn more from our encounters and exchanges. In so doing a way of approaching truth will take shape.

Seeing what my neighbour sees

You have probably seen the psychological test picture which some immediately perceive as a bonneted old woman with a pointed chin, who is looking down, and others see as a young girl, who is looking away to the left. (There is a copy in Douglas Gwyn's *Unmasking the Idols* [1989].)

A few years ago I read a newspaper report of an experiment in Mumbai (Bombay). In a slum area someone had set up a computer, securely fixed into an outside wall. No instructions were given to the children who gathered around this new marvel. After a little while some of them had worked out how to use the computer, and in the process they had applied their own words to what appeared on the screen. What the designers had no doubt intended as an hourglass, which appears on screen to indicate that the user must wait, the children were referring to as 'damru'.

A *damru* is a little hand-held drum. It has a narrow waist, just like an hourglass. This means that a travelling performer can easily hold it and shake it so that two tiny balls that are attached to it strike the two flat surfaces and provide a lively beat. Since the *damru* is associated with Lord Shiva, dancing his cosmic dance of creation, even this secular example of seeing the same thing differently leads one into a rich seam of reflection about time and the cosmos.

I recalled how on one occasion I took my friend, LMS, to Coventry cathedral. I showed him the inlaid floor of the Chapel of Unity and he surprised me by asking why there was a bell depicted in the mosaic. I had never noticed a bell and so I asked him what he meant. He pointed to what I knew was a chalice. On reflection I realised that I saw a chalice because I had been brought up in an Anglican family and as a child I had seen the Eucharistic cup Sunday by Sunday. I had, from an early age, made the connection between this and the cup that Jesus blessed at his last supper (Luke 22.17), and I made a further association with the cup of suffering that he asked the angel in the garden of Gethsemane to take from him (Luke 22.42). (This scene is wonderfully represented in Coventry cathedral's Gethsemane chapel.) For LMS none of these associations sprang to mind. His upbringing had probably involved seeing his mother or other Hindus animatedly ringing a handbell as part of the *arati* ceremony of light, scent and song. So the same outline on the floor appeared differently to each of us.

Now, on visits to the Chapel of Unity, I see the chalice in the mosaic as also a bell, and I reflect on the bell that calls (Christians) to worship as well as the bell that lets Goddess/God know that (Hindu) devotees are calling upon her/him.

These examples of seeing the same thing differently will connect with the discussion of truth(s) in chapter five. Even if there is a single truth, and even if we are all presented with it, whether in words or images, this cannot mean that we will all hear or see the same message. What I am urging is that the effort to hear and see what my neighbour hears and sees, or at least to be more aware of the difference between this and what I hear and see, is worthwhile. It not only brings us closer but it also deepens and extends my earlier perception of the truth. It reminds me to avoid making assumptions and helps me to become more conscious of my own cultural conditioning.

Recognising my own lenses

The approach to people's faiths and cultures that I outlined in chapter two requires each one of us as interfaith pilgrims to become more keenly aware of our individual and group histories, and of the constraints of our culture and language. We need to reflect, and to be doing so reflexively, as the way in which any of us relates to and comes to understand our neighbours is influenced by our own backgrounds and by how aware of these we are. We can adopt Jesus' image of removing the beam from our own eye in order to see the speck in our brother's (Matthew 7.3; Luke 6.41).

Of course 'Quaker' (and any other religious label that readers may apply to themselves or others) is only one of our many identities (as female, retired, Scottish, hard of hearing, a social worker, a student, a musician and so on). Our Quaker-ness is only one aspect of what we bring to any encounter, and we need to look investigatively at the deposits that the other key influences on us, and on the groups that we belong to, have left behind. (Some readers will have come across the Northern Friends Peace Board's publication (1997) *Who am I? Who are You?*

in which the contributors revealed some of the complexities of their identity.) We may feel too that it is not so much that Quakerism has helped to fashion us, but that at some point we looked at what we already were, or aspired to become, and noticed that 'Quaker' appeared to fit it.

But, however we perceive our relationship with being Quaker, this is – by our own admission – the religious aspect of our identity. It is how we see ourselves, and maybe how others pigeonhole us. It is, therefore, particularly appropriate to ask ourselves what being a Quaker means. (Some readers may wish to interrogate another religious label at this point! Methodist? Muslim? Agnostic?)

In addition to a geographical diversity, related to historical developments among Friends worldwide, Britain Yearly Meeting is itself plural. 'Christocentric' and 'Universalist' designate two distinguishable emphases, both evident in articles and correspondence in *The Friend*. Some Friends – Christocentric Friends – share with (other) Christians a conviction, or at least a feeling that we should be convinced, of Jesus' unique status as divine Saviour and human teacher. Other Friends – Universalists – know, and know passionately, that no single faith has a monopoly of truth.

How do we characterise our own Quaker-ness? How do our convictions and hunches affect our responses to others? Before embarking on interfaith explorations we can give ourselves some more jolts towards self-awareness. Try out the aliens exercise that Robert Jackson, one of my colleagues, recommends for students of all ages setting out to understand faith communities (1989; Jackson and Killingley 1988: 24-26). You are an alien from another planet visiting earth on the day which we earthlings know to be December 25th. You report back what you see as you look into a living room in which stands (what we UK earthlings know to be) a Christmas tree surrounded by presents. Do conifers run households of human slaves? Do earthlings worship trees? Now imagine yourself as a Martian, or as a Muslim, or a devotee of Sathya Sai Baba (the South Indian teacher revered by devotees as God in human form) visiting the local Friends Meeting for Worship on a Sunday morning. What is the meaning of the circle of chairs, the table, the vase of flowers, the various postures and facial expressions?

We can also try seeing ourselves through the eyes of a novelist – Iris Murdoch's family included several Quakers, and in *The Philosopher's Pupil* she offers us an imagined account of people's unexpressed thoughts during a meeting for worship (1983). So too does Margaret Drabble in *The Witch of Exmoor* (1996), and Leila Dutt's *Rubik's Cube* provides a fictional description of Quaker activity in a university city (1984).

Or look at what anthropologists have written – our Friend, Peter Collins for example, on 'plaining' (1996). He suggests that it is not so much the peace testimony, or affirmation of the inner light, but pursuit of what is plain that has, historically at least, unified Friends. This plainness could be as unassailable for Friends as any ritual, and it evolved as a plainness primarily distinguishing us from Church of England norms of architecture, priesthood and ceremonial. His anthropological observation helps me to understand more sharply the Quaker tradition that I had taken for granted.

Certainly our plainness in worship – the absence of image, sound and action, let alone colour – is likely to be the primary impression of visiting neighbours from other faith communities. True, Sikh practice marks a reformist step away from the detailed devotions to deities in Hindu tradition. But any Quaker visitor to the Sikhs' gurdwara is struck by the special ways in which Sikhs show their respect to the Guru Granth Sahib, the volume of scripture, enthroned on its imposing stand, and visitors cannot help but notice what we might perceive to be

Christmas-style decorations adorning the prayer hall.

We may agree or disagree with a novelist's portrayal or anthropologist's analysis. In so doing we examine ourselves and our Quaker-ness, and how it appears to neighbours of other faiths, in a new way.

Another way of becoming aware of our own cultural norms is through interaction with others and reflecting on their apparent misapprehensions. Let us turn our attention from Britain Yearly Meeting to British breakfasts. When I was much younger Annie, my French pen-friend, came to stay with me and asked for marmalade at tea time. Years later LMS (whom I mentioned above) stayed with us and ate his bread and marmalade with his cereal. On these occasions I learned to recognise my particular English assumptions about the daily sequencing of food (in this case marmalade) as appropriate to a particular time of day, and to a particular stage in one particular meal, for what they were – local conventions.

For Friends truth and truthfulness have a non-negotiable centrality – of a different order from rules about marmalade. But this does not prevent us noting how our expressions of truth can strike our neighbour. One person's truthfulness is another's insensitive rudeness, or hurtful, unfeeling literality. When I speak of my father's second wife I may call her my step-mother, and when I introduce my husband's daughter I may call her my step-daughter. My Sikh and Hindu friends and family feel uneasy or protest that I should omit the 'step' and simply say 'mother' and 'daughter'. Similarly children are encouraged to call their cousins their brothers and sisters. An Indian friend once pointed out to me that there are two kinds of truth – literal truth and the truth of intention – in these cases the intention of affirming love and relationship as mother and daughter, or as siblings, which is of far greater import than literality.

Listening for my neighbour's concern

Given our very different cultural conditioning, it is not sur-
prising that we have different priorities and anxieties which we
regard as part and parcel of religion generally. When, in the
1980s, I asked some Hindus what they wanted schools to teach
in religious education about Hinduism the answers were not
what I had anticipated. I had imagined that they might mention
particular 'beliefs' or 'practices' that fitted with my concep-
tion of what a religion is. (I would have benefited from reading
chapter two of this book!) Instead of asking for particular
stories of the gods or commending instruction about *karma* or
reincarnation, they said, 'language'. They wished that schools
would provide Gujarati or Hindi lessons. This set me thinking
about the inseparability of religion and language, and about the
different ways in which my friends and I were using and understanding the word 'Hinduism'.

Another concern that surfaced – and Christians, Muslims and
Sikhs who have been brought up in South Asia have expressed the
same concern to me so many times over the years – was that children should be encouraged to address others, and to refer to
them, with the language of respect and affection. They expressed
hurt that young people growing up in Britain were less ready to
use relationship terms such as 'Aunty' than, say, 'Shanta' (first
name) or 'Mrs Pande'. The former way of addressing and referring to an older woman by just her first name sounded
disrespectful and over-familiar. The latter (title and surname)
sounded too coldly formal. For parents the fact that children
did not learn particular facts was much less distressing than
hearing them using 'English' ways of talking to people and about
them. As it happens, only the day before rewriting this para-
graph I heard an Indian woman, a Friend in Residence at
Woodbrooke Quaker Study Centre, trying to explain to another
Friend in Residence how unthinkable it would be in India for a

younger person to address an older person by using her given name, eg Kamla or Mary, rather than as 'Aunty'. She recalled how in school she used to be reprimanded if she called pupils who were only a year older than her by name rather than addressing them as 'Didi' (older sister) or 'Bhaia' (older brother). These terms convey affection, respect for seniority and immediately confirm relationship. They seal a bond.

Hindus have expressed their hurt to me at hearing a son or daughter say 'Your friend called' rather than 'Uncle or Aunty called'. This is for two reasons – 'friend' suggests a greater distance between people than do relationship words such as 'uncle'. (As Friends, with our own understanding of 'friend', we may be surprised to hear this perception.) Also 'your' implies that this is an individual friendship, whereas every relationship involves the whole family, not just one member or one generation. The person whom my mother calls 'sister' I will call 'aunty' or 'masi' (mother's sister), not 'your friend'.

I have laboured these related points partly because of the frequency with which South Asians have drawn my attention to it. They may say (depending on their background) that this is part of being Hindu/Sikh/Muslim. The fact that we may distinguish culture from religion more sharply than they do is to miss the point that I am making here. I have also given this as an example because it marks a disjunction, not only with prevailing secular western practice, but also with a deliberate Quaker stand on the use of names and Quakers' positive valuation of the word 'friend'. Our conversation with neighbours of 'other faiths' (and with South Asian Friends) will benefit by our indicating to them that we are aware of this difference. We could, for instance, make a point of at least enquiring how they would really prefer us or our children to address them. Also, in line with the thrust of this chapter, if we pause to ponder the implications of a fundamental cultural difference, we can see the limitations and quirkiness of our own assumptions and stances. I have come to have a stronger sense of connectedness and to value the insight that my friend is my sister. At the same time I can reappraise and value afresh an American's or a fellow Britisher's tribute to his wife or his father as his best friend.

Two conversations with Christian (Catholic and Protestant) neighbours reminded me that Christians too have concerns and priorities which are less widespread among people of faith than they assume or would like to be the case. Both conversations were to do with Sundays. The first took place at the time when Sunday trading was a matter of public debate just before Sunday trading restrictions were lifted. My neighbour asked me whether he could summon the support of Hindus and Sikhs for his stand against relaxing the law, as they must, as people of faith, have similar views about keeping one day holy. He realised that this might not be a Sunday in the case of other religious traditions. But he assumed that Hindus and Sikhs would respect the same principle, and he was not expecting me to point out, as I in fact did, that Sikhs and Hindus do not share Jewish regard for the Sabbath as a day of rest, nor Christian respect for the Lord's Day, nor even an Islamic observance of a weekly day for congregational prayer.

I probably – insensitively – bored him with a potted lecture on a Hindu view of time in which no one day of the week was specially set apart by divine commandment or common consent, but in which different individuals might mark particular days of the week or lunar month by a particular observance (often a *vrat* ie vow, involving abstinence from certain foods) for certain periods of time. Moreover, I must have said, Hindu understanding of the stages of life meant that working and providing for the family were appropriate priorities until their children had grown up. Yes, time for devotion had its place, and for many Hindus this means daily worship at the domestic shrine as well as in the sense of devoting one's old age to worship, meditation and scriptural reading, rather than as a weekly requirement throughout one's life, to be marked by a weekly day of 'rest'.

The second conversation involved my neighbours' children's Church of England secondary school. Here, as they told me, the school's earlier criterion of Christian commitment for a family's eligibility had been extended to a quota of families from other faith communities. Christian parents' commitment was evident in their weekly attendance at church. If Hindus wished to enrol their children they should attend the temple more often. I pointed out that for Hindus such a criterion is more problematic. For a start one can argue (as I often do) that 'Christian' and 'Hindu' are not strictly comparable, since the nub of being a Christian is (from a dominant Christian standpoint) one's 'faith', whereas 'Hindu' is in origin a more geographical and cultural designation – more like 'European'. This being so, 'commitment' is a problematic notion. Even if one does not follow this train of thought, and one decides that a Hindu's commitment can be measured in terms of devotional practice, there is no inherently Hindu expectation that this devotional practice will be congregational or that it will require weekly visits to a public place of worship, let alone to one temple in particular.

So, what appeared to my Christian neighbours as intrinsically religious priorities, which would have ready parallels in other communities, were in fact less close to Hindus' concerns than they had assumed. (Of course Jewish belief and practice would provide a much closer parallel – and indeed it was synagogue and Sabbath [Shabbat] which provided early Christians with their framework.) Instead 'being religious shows in your food' was how a Hindu twelve year old aptly identified for me the hallmark of the devout Hindu (see Nesbitt 1999b). She was thinking especially of Ba, her grandmother, whose religious discipline was Pushtimarg (the 'way of grace'). In keeping with her gurus' teaching and example Ba ate only strictly vegetarian food, and this excluded onion and garlic (associated with lust), and she would accept only food that had been prepared by a Pushtimargi. This is not the case for all Hindus, but Ba's grand-daughter's comment articulates a much more widespread Hindu acceptance that spiritual progress requires vegetarianism and periodic fasting.

This Hindu girl mentioned the significance of 'food' as an indicator of devotion, not to distinguish Hindu criteria from Christian ones, but to distinguish Hindus from Sikhs, whose commitment would show not 'in their food' but 'in their hair'. This is because, especially for Khalsa (initiated) Sikhs, one's hair is God's gift and, as such, is not to be shortened or removed. To do so would be to disobey the tenth Guru's command.

I am not suggesting that the Church of England school should examine its Sikh applicants' hair or its Hindu applicants' diet. In any case these are contested issues within the communities concerned. However, these examples serve to remind us that interfaith discussion, religious education, and policies in a multifaith society can be mistaken in too readily focusing on certain selected aspects and details of life as if they are uniformly applicable and important across the board.

Asking my neighbour's question: Who is my Guru?

On several occasions I have been invited to share insights with (other) Christian groups. Some of these groups have been concerned with dialogue, some with mission. I find myself urging Christians to consider whether they are more concerned with answers to their own, Christian questions, or with listening for their neighbour's question? Is their neighbour really concerned to know 'Who is my Saviour?' Do these words even make sense to her?

Then, when we hear our neighbour's question, do we accept it as a gift and allow it to open up and affirm the truth within our own tradition and experience? And can we also accept that our question may serve our neighbour as an instrument for opening up and affirming her tradition's truth, rather than propelling her into a new (Christian) allegiance?

What follows is an example, which I have shared with several church groups, from a visit that I made to Punjab in 1984. 'Which Guru do you believe in?' This question came from a Sikh villager and I knew I had to answer it to the best of my ability. I did not know enough Punjabi to go into carefully nuanced – evasive – answers. I replied briefly 'Isa Masih' [Jesus Christ]. I will never know what if anything this conveyed to my Sikh neighbour, but it has left me pondering ever since in what ways Jesus is, can be, or is not a Guru for me or, more generally, for Quakers. Below are my reflections. Anyone wishing to pursue this idea further could start by reading the thoughts of Freeman (2000) and Thangaraj (1994).

In widespread western usage 'guru' has come to be a slightly tongue in cheek word for an expert. You can have fashion gurus and food gurus. For centuries in Hindu society a guru has meant a teacher, and very often a spiritual master whose followers would owe him total devotion. Listen to the prayer with which hundreds of young Hindus begin their weekly classes, run by Hindu organisations, up and down the UK:

Brahma is Guru, Vishnu is Guru;
The supreme absolute is Guru, I bow to my Gurus.

They may learn that the Guru is more important than God, because without a Guru one cannot reach God. As one primary school girl wrote in her notebook at a weekly class organised by local devotees of ISKCON (the Hare Krishna movement), 'If we didn't have a Guru we wouldn't know about Krishna'.

Much as the Sikh community has emerged from within the wider Hindu tradition and become distinctively itself, so the standard Sikh understanding of Guru (best kept capitalised when written in the roman alphabet) is more specific than the broader Hindu (lower case) one. For Sikhs, 'Guru' refers not to teachers more generally, and not to a potentially infinite number of spiritual guides, but to the ten founder-masters of the Panth (Sikhs' term for the Sikh community). The line of Gurus started with Martin Luther's near contemporary, Guru Nanak, and ended with Guru Gobind Singh who died, 17 years after George Fox, in 1708.

Accounts of the human Gurus' lives illustrate the self-surrender of devotees – in fact Guru Nanak chose as successor not one of his two sons, but a faithful follower, who passed a series of tests of his obedient devotion. At the same time the Guru identified with his faithful followers. In one story Guru Nanak's skin is scarred by the thorns that his distant follower is carrying (an interesting inversion of some saintly Christians' hands and feet bleeding with the stigmata of Christ on the cross).

Quakers respect the reported teachings of the itinerant and controversial rabbi, Jesus: many Christians worship him as the Messiah (anointed one) and as God incarnate, a 'person' of Christians' Trinity. Wherever we place ourselves in this spectrum of belief, we can try refreshing our relationship with Jesus/Christ, and our understanding of this, by contemplating him as Guru/guru.

For my relationship with Jesus as guru to come fully alive I am helped by pondering what Hindus and Sikhs mean by 'guru'. For example, Sikhs' explanation of Guru as the remover of darkness, the enlightener, turns my thoughts to the opening verses of St John's gospel, concerning the Word which was incarnated as Jesus. Here we read that 'The light shines in the darkness, and the darkness has not overcome it' (John 1.5) and 'I am the light of the world' (John 8.12). What do these claims mean? Is Jesus too a Guru, an enlightener, in the sense of dispelling ignorance?

There is another aspect of my Sikh friend's question. Before they enter any room in which the sacred volume has been installed Sikhs remove their footwear and cover their heads. This is because the scripture, the Guru Granth Sahib, is also the living Guru, the successor to the ten human Gurus. Accordingly, if you go to a gurdwara, or to the room in a private house in which the Guru Granth Sahib is kept, you will find that the volume lies open on a cushioned stand, with a canopy above it and an attendant waving a traditional fan made of yak or horse tail hair. This is how a retainer would (before the age of electric fans and air conditioning) have fanned an enthroned prince or a revered spiritual teacher — and so it symbolises the Guru's authority. Every day the volume is opened at random, and the verse at the top of the left hand page is read out and accepted as the guru's 'order' for the day. Each night the scriptures are ceremonially laid to rest — often in a room resembling a bedroom.

So this villager's question also sets me wondering whether any scripture is my teacher. Do I need a sacred text as well as a human teacher? Is this the Bible? The Gospels? Do I in effect regard a great mass of writings (my personal canon) as potential Gurus — poetry, devotional anthologies, accounts of spiritual journeys, translations of Buddhist and Hindu literature? Does this high regard mean treating the physical publication with respect? Is the regular practice of random opening of my book-Guru for guidance a gift which Sikhs' relationship with the Guru offers for the spiritual deepening of my own life?

Nearly twenty years on I reply, 'Yes, Jesus in Christian scripture is my Guru, but I have other gurus too. The gospel Jesus beckons and tantalises. He commands and he stays silent. He loves inclusively.' And I can catch some of his words, speaking directly to me, in the writing of his chosen followers, Matthew, Mark, Luke and John – and Thomas (see for example: http://www.goodnewsinc.net/othbooks/thomas.html).

My Sikh acquaintance's question has reactivated my engagement with what I took for granted. So too did a glimpse of a Punjabi translation of one of the Christian gospels.

Looking at my neighbour's translation

Dipping into this translation I found the word 'gurdwara' used to translate 'synagogue'. Gurdwara – literally gateway of the Guru – is the term for a Sikh place of worship, or more precisely for any place in which the Guru Granth Sahib has been installed. Here people gather to soak in the word of the Guru, spoken and sung, and to offer free vegetarian hospitality (the *langar* meal) to allcomers. Once again my thoughts were set in motion as I puzzled over ways in which synagogue and gurdwara were alike or different, and pondered the motivation of the translator in making the strange biblical institution familiar to Sikh readers through this choice of word.

And what, I wondered next, of our Meeting Houses and Meetings for Worship? In what way are they or could they be gurdwaras? Sikhs emphasise the fact that the seating arrangement – everyone cross-legged on the floor, men on one side usually and women on the other – demonstrates equality of all, regardless of gender or relative status or seniority. Visually the focus is unmistakably the enthroned scripture and this provides the content of corporate worship. What is our apparent or real focus in Meeting? Is it evident to the visitor? Is it the vase of studiously unarranged flowers and foliage on the table in the centre of the room? Is it the generally unopened Bible or *Quaker faith & practice*? What fills our minds during 'worship'? Is our 'listening to the light' (to quote Jim Pym 1999) in the silence in any way a similar experience to immersing oneself as a Sikh in the poignant melody of the Gurus' hymns? And what about that *langar* – should we have more, not fewer, bring and share lunches? I once heard the ecumenist, Donald Nicholl, affirming the importance of conviviality – in its underlying Latin sense of feasting together, rather than mere matiness – for bonding together people of faith(s).

Using my neighbour's concepts: polishing and refining

Two of my favourite concepts – both originally Hindu – for teasing out fresh insights into human behaviour (not least ours as Quakers) are *sanskar* and *darshan*. We will look at *sanskar* in this chapter and at *darshan* in chapter four. Both are words firmly rooted in the ancient language of Sanskrit, and each at first sight has two meanings which from an outside perspective seem rather different from each other. In each case, by looking for the unifying concept underlying the apparently dissimilar applications, I search my own experience further and feel liberated from my English-formed concepts in my exchanges with others.

Let me give some concrete examples of *sanskar*. In the years before my step-daughter's marriage my husband and I used to discuss the responsibility of parents for arranging their children's marriages. We would quickly reach an impasse. This was because, while he acknowledged that marriage to someone, perhaps newly arrived from India, whom she did not know, might end unhappily, he knew that as a parent he must ensure that she 'settled' as soon as possible. Both of us knew that many love-marriages were similarly unsatisfactory. At the same time I accepted, on the basis of my experience over many years, that even in the British-reared generation of young people of

South Asian family background, many 'assisted' marriages did 'work'. I knew that if a young woman's family do not take the initiative in finding a partner for her she may remain – in traditional South Asian terms anyway – unsettled and a burden, psychologically at least, on her parents. Yet acting as a responsible parent in this respect went against my grain. Our divergent attitudes were, my husband patiently explained, the result of our different *sanskars*. In this instance I can translate *sanskar* as conditioning or a profound influence on my life.

To take another example from the family, but illustrating another area of *sanskar*'s meaning. When a relative became a 'born again Christian' my husband maintained that he was nevertheless, beyond doubt, a Hindu. While I insisted that the individual concerned could determine the most appropriate religious label for himself by what he decided to believe and how he proceeded to worship, my husband was no less adamant that anyone who had had a *mundan* (the head shaving which for many Hindu boys marks their transition from infancy) and also had a Hindu marriage is without a shadow of a doubt a Hindu. These life-cycle rites are also *sanskars*.

Investigation of the Sanskrit (literally 'polished language' – a word from the same root as *sanskar*) clarifies the conceptual linkage between formative impressions and rites of passage. The Sanskrit word *samskara* means polishing, refining, making perfect – through both one's early conditioning and one's ritual processing. Culture itself – in Hindi *sanskriti* – is what polishes and refines the raw animal material of humankind. With this in mind my understanding of 'others' is helped by taking a long analytical look at my own *sanskars* as well as recognising more holistically my neighbours' deep-seated attitudes and their ritualised processing. I become aware as I do this that interfaith dialogue might be less wobbly if the focus was on our *sanskars* in the fullest, profoundest sense rather than (more narrowly, and

I suspect often superficially) on theology and religious oratory.

In conclusion

I am not for a moment suggesting that in order to proceed with understanding our neighbours and fellow pilgrims better we need to master a set of concepts for which English provides no ready equivalent. But, from my own experience, I can commend a process of listening and watching out for our neighbours' categories and then teasing out all the relevance we can for understanding our own experience as much as theirs. This doesn't mean that we need to be forever delving into dictionaries or learning unfamiliar scripts. Just listen to the way in which our neighbours express in English what matters to them. Is it the way that we would have put things? Can it help us to review our own lives through slightly different lenses? Are they using English words for underlying concepts which only partly overlap with those which these words more usually convey to us? By so doing we may all be confusing ourselves rather than helping each other's exploration. For example, the fact that a Hindu or Sikh uses English words, such as 'God', 'priest' and 'prayer' may obscure rather than illuminate our understanding unless we listen attentively.

This is because she may be using 'God' for a living saint who incarnates God, or a Sikh may be using 'priest' for the person who is publicly reading the scriptures, or who looks after the gurdwara, even though there is no priestly caste nor sacrament of ordination and there is no professional group of specialists who have been trained to be pastors or specialists in ritual or doctrine. My neighbour may use 'prayer' to refer to reading and repeating sacred words, whereas it is petition ('dear Lord, please help me...') which comes to my mind when I hear the word 'prayer'. We need to be looking beyond our usual understandings of these words, and of many others, if we are to be alert explorers of interfaith terrain.

Treating my neighbour as myself, in any but a superficial way, means looking at her lenses and mine and trying to look through her lenses. It means listening for questions and concerns and looking for new richness in our apparently shared language. By so doing we open up for ourselves new vistas of understanding. With this in mind, worship will be the focus for chapter four: for interfaith pilgrims worship signals opportunities for furthering our experiential, experimental approach to truth.

CHAPTER FOUR

Worship

Sunday by Sunday Quakers gather for a 'Meeting for Worship'. 'Worship' is one of the first words that comes to mind when we encounter the distinctively religious behaviour of people of faith. We use it for activities as diverse as private, silent meditation and public, corporate chanting, singing and clapping, and for liturgies involving sequences of movement, sharing of food and drink, the burning of incense and splendid, colourful spectacle. I shall be sharing ways in which our own worship as interfaith pilgrims – and Quaker ones in particular – may be fed by a receptive exploration of other ways of worship. Not only our weekly hour of worship together, but also our everyday experience, can be challenged and enriched.

This was my discovery, as I got to know my neighbour in the adjoining corner house to mine. Savitaben is a Hindu, her family roots are in Gujarat (India) and she grew up in Kenya. I entitled my poem 'Semi-detached', not just because we lived in next door semis but because this adjective described my own state of being part observer, part involved.

> The scent of sandalwood drifts from my neighbour's door;
> The breeze, already sweet with roses and mown grass,
> Shares out the fragrance of her daily prayer.
> Morning and evening, through our common wall,

Her handbell tells of faithful offerings
To God in many guises on the shelf
Which serves as shrine, and as I pass her window
I glance in, to glimpse the wick alight,
And light and lightness lift my heart.
This is Savita's ministry, enhanced
With tasty dishes, delicately spiced and gladly shared.
But, on my side, Savita finds
No light, no bell, no lingering incense and no
    festooned God,
No corner kept for reverence, feet unshod,
Only, perhaps, some neighbourly goodwill.
(Nesbitt 1999c)

A Jewish writer provides a prose quotation to introduce the following series of reflections on the gifts which worship brings to our interfaith pilgrimage towards truth.

The pure idea can serve only a few rare individuals –
theologians, philosophers, if you will. The truth – to
be felt by most of us – must put on a garb. There
must be rite, legend, ceremony, visible form.
(Schindler 1988: xiii)

With these words Alexander Schindler prefaced Daniel B. Syme's *The Jewish Home, A Guide to Jewish Living*. They could equally have introduced guides to Christian, Hindu and so many other ways of living.

In similar vein I heard Keith Ward (Regius Professor of Divinity in the University of Oxford) point out in a lecture that 'religious traditions live mainly by images and metaphors'. This being so, he said, 'the question of theoretical truth may indeed be less important in practice than the personal efficacy of the images in leading one from egoism toward union with the reality of compassion and bliss'.

Accordingly, this chapter presents worship, and especially the images and metaphors that interpenetrate worship, as ways towards truth (that 'reality of compassion and bliss') and towards our fuller engagement with it.

Quaker reservations

However, we may well feel that in respect of our style of worship, at least, Quakers part company with most of our neighbours. In chapter three I alluded to Peter Collins' argument, on the basis of careful observation, that Quakers can be characterised as 'plaining' (1996). We aspire to and commend plainness, whether this means a lack of ceremony or an unadorned meeting place, or even a certain roughness in 'speaking our truth'. This plainness has historically been plainness in reaction to (in particular) Anglican worship and church buildings. And silence and emptiness in turn have become respected convention (and a symbol) that defines Quakers every bit as much as a multi-sensory liturgy or a more complex style of architecture expresses the ethos and beliefs of other religious communities.

In chapter two I referred to dimensions of faiths and to a Quaker tendency to select those dimensions of other faiths (such as their 'mysticism') which we can most comfortably affirm within our Quaker tradition. But being open and affirmative to our neighbours' spirituality requires us to approach with sympathetic interest the time-honoured practices and distinctive apparatus that their ways of worshipping involve. It is all too easy for us Quakers to assume a) that our own ways preclude ritual and b) that – if we are visiting a mosque or a temple – practical considerations and 'common sense' allow us to dispense with, say, Muslims' or Hindus' right ordering. (Yes, let us not forget that we too have a religious jargon.)

It can be challenging to take my religious education students on visits to local places of worship, and every bit as challenging to accompany other Friends. Independent-minded logic may suggest to one of the party, who has difficulty in bending over to remove footwear outside the worship area, that the divine principle will have no objection to his/her going inside, just a few inches, to perch on that seat at the back to untie laces or unbuckle sandals. But what the ruffled member of the congregation sees is somebody offending (they hope from ignorance rather than defiance) against a basic rule of conduct.

The plain, common sense Quaker in us may warm to these two stories from the *janam sakhis* (popular retellings of episodes in the life of Guru Nanak). Guru Nanak visited Makkah as a pilgrim (although he was not a Muslim), and he appalled the local Muslim authority by proceeding to lie down to sleep with his feet pointing in the direction of the *kaba*, which all Muslims face, wherever in the world they are praying. (Interestingly, our Friend, Marjorie Sykes, related an almost identical story about a Hindu woman saint in relation to a shrine.) In reply to the Muslim's rebuke, Guru Nanak requested him to move his feet so that they pointed in a direction 'where God is not' (McLeod 1980: 52). Rather similarly, on a visit to Hindus' holy river Ganga (Ganges), he watched the pilgrims throwing water towards the rising sun as a gesture of refreshing the souls of their deceased ancestors, and he then began to throw water towards the north-west (McLeod 1980: 83-84). Shocked, someone challenged him: 'Are you a Muslim?' (Makkah is north-west from the Ganga.) Guru Nanak explained that if the water that they were throwing could travel thousands of miles to the sun, then he could water his fields in Punjab, which was a great deal closer. Since this was clearly impossible, so too (no doubt he intended his audience to conclude) the pilgrims' ritual water-throwing must be even more futile.

In a similar vein we may think too of Jesus contravening Sabbath law in order to heal the sick or his anger with the moneylenders in the temple in Jerusalem (Matthew 21.12-13; Mark 11.15-18), or we may recall the less than reverent behaviour of George Fox inside churches. Arguably the reformer is entitled to overthrow the apple-cart of his/her *own* community. For us Quakers it may be easier to applaud Jesus' non-conformity, or the Guru's visual challenges to devotees to question their rituals, than to make sure in a gurdwara that we are not causing needless offence to Sikhs by sitting with our feet pointing towards the Guru Granth Sahib.

But without doubt any initiative we may take in learning from our neighbour requires us, as interfaith pilgrims, to respect our neighbour's expectations and sensitivities. The pilgrim does not vandalise in Puritan Reformist zeal but bows her head! In this way the pilgrim in us needs to set the iconoclast to one side, so that we are open to whatever insights our neighbours' worship unfolds. Roger Hooker, an Anglican interfaith pioneer, shared the discovery that his efforts, as a Protestant, to understand Hindu worship brought him a more sympathetic understanding of his Orthodox and Roman Catholic co-religionists. Marcus Braybrooke, another Anglican priest, has devoted his life for over thirty years to interfaith activity. He shares his discovery that 'as a follower of one path, my contact with other traditions has helped me to discover both new riches in my own faith tradition and new experiences which I have subsequently integrated into my own spiritual practice' (1999: 13).

So, however we conceive of the relationship between Meeting for Worship and more liturgical or more sensory ways of worship, I am suggesting that we would be ill-advised to deliberately disregard any windows on truth that our neighbour's worship can offer us.

What is worship?

Because an 'act of collective worship' is statutory in state schools colleagues in my field – religious education – have exercised their minds on this question. Perhaps this has contributed to my own sense of worship as a wide, generous, embracing word, accommodating both the understandings that I am about to quote. Our Friend John Punshon has affirmed that:

> To worship it is essential for us to come to the knowledge that we are each very dear to God. There is no other starting point. (1987)

The religious educationist, Peggy Morgan, has suggested:

> It is not necessary to be relating to a personal God to worship. Worship defined as 'the acknowledgement of what is of ultimate worth' includes the Buddhist who acknowledges…a transpersonal state, the state of enlightenment or Nirvana. (1989)

Worship is certainly what I witness on my visits to a local mosque with students, when we are privileged to be present during the midday prayer. The Hindi novelist, Munshi Premchand, evokes the impact on the 'outsider' of Muslim *namaz* (prayer) in his short story 'Idgah'. He describes the conclusion to Ramadan, the month of fasting, in a small Indian village:

> Rows upon rows of worshippers as far as the eye can see…Tens of thousands bow their heads in prostration, everyone together stands up, together they bow and together they sit on their heels, as if thousands of electric lights are being turned on and off…their hearts filled with religious awe, elation and spiritual joy, as if one thread of brotherhood threaded all these souls on a single string.
> (Premchand no date: 50)

In this chapter I will be sharing, from my own interfaith

pilgrimage, reflections on words and images which arise from my experience of worship in another tradition – in this case the Hindu tradition. I will then look at what Meeting for Worship can mean for the interfaith pilgrim.

Darshan

Somewhere in India the bus pulls to a halt beside a wayside shrine. A passenger gets down, stands with his palms pressed respectfully together, turns back and boards the bus again. He has in that minute 'taken *darshan*'.

Darshan (the older Sanskrit form of this word is transliterated as *darsana*) is, like *sanskar* (in chapter four), a word which has at first sight two distinct meanings. In books on Hinduism the term is sometimes translated as 'school of philosophy'. Less formal and exclusive-sounding are renderings such as point of view or perspective. But, in everyday speech, Hindus are much less likely to be discussing classical philosophy than to be referring to the exchange of glances between devotee and deity. *Darshan* is the benediction of glimpsing divinity, however fleetingly, and of knowing that the divine gaze has fallen upon one. Probably 'audience' – as in the phrase 'an audience with the Pope' – comes closest in English, but 'audience' is an originally aural metaphor, while *darshan* is visual.

Perhaps as Quakers we find it more difficult to conceive of an exchange of glances between ourselves and the ultimate than of an exchange of words or indeed of silences. *Darshan* may appeal to us more easily as a concept that allows for an intellectual perception of the truth from infinite, non-exclusive, angles. We may find, however, that the popular everyday Hindu experience of *darshan* further validates our memories of significant encounters with inspirational individuals, with works of art or with places of great natural beauty in the course of our own spiritual journeying.

The divine gaze can be so dangerously powerful that humans can bear only a momentary exposure. This is why the curtains over the Srinath image in Leytonstone's Srinathji temple are drawn back for only a few moments at a time to allow the devotee to gaze at the *murti* (image) in the shrine. Can our meditation accommodate a God whose gaze is so potent?

Puja

Puja is worship which involves offering to one's chosen form of deity some devotional music, incense, water, flowers, fruits and sweets. This takes place daily in little domestic shrines – in boxroom temples and cupboard temples, in corners set aside in bedrooms, living rooms and kitchens – in Hindu households everywhere.

In her novel *Amritvela*, Leena Dhingra evokes a woman's low-key, daily domestic *puja*:

> Bibiji is in her puja room, performing the daily ritual she has done all her life since childhood…each of the brass figures will be taken down from its place, bathed, wiped and then returned…Then each of the deities will have a single flower placed in front of it…After the offering of each flower, Bibiji will join her hands in reverent salutation before offering the next…when all this has been meticulously done, Bibiji will light the incense and pray. (1988: 97-98)

As I daily receive, offer, receive back and share out my day – my daily bread – the transforming give and take of *puja* becomes clearer to me.

Do I need solitude to be in my sacred space? Do I need fellow worshippers? Do I need apparatus – flowers on the table, a holy book? A yoga mat? Should I be setting up a dedicated votive space at home – can it be a non-theistic shrine? Pebbles from a beach, a freshly cut flower, a photograph?

Arati

Hindu worship often closes with *arati*. This involves standing at the shrine and reverently, yet enthusiastically, circling a lighted lamp – often on a round metal tray – clockwise in front of a saint's or deity's image, to the sounds of singing and the ringing of a handbell. The air is fragrant with incense. Worshippers disperse only after passing their hands over the flame and then over their eyes and heads and, finally, sharing fruit, nuts or sweet-meats that have, along with flowers, been offered in worship. For Guru Nanak this daily devotion provided the inspiration for a poem, here inadequately in English translation:

> The heavens are your salver,
> The sun and moon your lamps,
> The galaxy of stars are your scattered pearls,
> The sandal woods are your incense,
> The breezes are the fan waved in worship,
> The flowers of the forests
> Lie at your feet as offerings.
> What wonderful *arati* this is,
> O you who destroy fear!
> Unstruck music is the sound of your temple drums.
>> (Adi Granth: 13, Rag Dhanasri. See Singh 1995: 140 for another rendering.)

'Unstruck music' – all music involves the impact of one thing on another. With percussion and stringed instruments this is obvious, but wind instruments, too, are silent until air is blown into them. So 'unstruck music' is a deliberate contradiction in terms – a paradox. Is it the sound of silence, the music of God's name for those who forget outside distractions in meditation? Is this Pythagoras's 'harmony of the spheres'? Is it the sound of one hand clapping?

Is Meeting for Worship filled with 'unstruck music'?

Prashad

Prasada or *prashad* means grace, God's grace, and is the food that has been offered in the temple and which is then distributed as God's abundant leftovers, God's gift to all who enter. My husband often returns from the temple with bananas and apples, or a mix of almonds, pistachios, large crystals of white sugar, cardamoms and wizened green sultanas. During two periods of nine days and nights known as Navratre (or Navaratri) in April and October *prashad* arrives daily from the temple.

So, in our house the muesli has caused the occasional overnight visitor to enquire where we bought it. Accustomed over the years to the periodic mixing in of some of the *prashad* I am glad to be reminded of the oddity of its content. Preparing breakfast gives me pause for thought – food as a sign of grace and plenty, for which to feel deeply thankful, muesli symbolising a culturally diverse household or a reminder of my quirkily lumpy individual spiritual mix?

Mantra

'Om bhur bhuvah svah tatsavitur varenyam bhargo devasya dhimahi dhiyo yo nah prachodayat.' This is a *mantra*, and these are the Sanskrit words which embellish our living room clock – a gift from Leicester. In 1986, as a 'participant observer' doing some field work at a large Hindu gathering, I found myself, cross-legged, in one of many family groups in a Leicester park, each sitting around a fire that had been kindled in a small, four-sided metal container. We were all reciting the words of the ancient Gayatri mantra the required 108 times, as we fed the flames with spoonfuls of ghee and aromatic herbs.

Since that event this ancient Sanskrit prayer for enlightenment has often run through my head – sometimes in Meeting for Worship. I do not understand its literal meaning, nor do most Hindus. But they know for sure that the words are good, and that they are powerful, and that reciting them brings peace of mind.

Hindus have shared with me other mantras, other Sanskrit formulae, which bring them serenity and make the day go better (or, in the case of one lad whom I interviewed, help you jump higher in high jump). In his case the words were those of the *mahamantra* (great mantra) that is recited by devotees of Krishna:

> Hare Rama Hare Rama Rama Rama Hare Hare
> Hare Krishna Hare Krishna Krishna Krishna Hare Hare.

On wooden beads, or with every breath, others invoke Shiva or Sathya Sai Baba. Influenced by Hindu practice, a Christian writer, Marcus Braybrooke, suggests that if we practise 'slowly repeating a sacred word or inspirational phrase' it can calm us and serve as a 'safety line to grasp when we are too angry or upset to think of anything to say to the divine' (2001: 49).

A mantra is like a seed which will germinate and grow within the heart. All that is required of the devotee is not intellectual understanding, but humble, constant repetition. In Quaker silence can I let these words – or any words – soak into me, take a hold and grow in this way? Perhaps the Jesus prayer: 'Lord Jesus Christ, Son of God, have mercy on me'? Or a verse of Christian scripture: 'Into thy hands I commit my spirit' (Luke 23.46)? Or 'Not my will, but thine, be done' (Luke 22.42)? Is this blind superstition or open-minded tentative experiment in the process of discovering my truth?

Are words a means of stilling my mind, of regrouping my scattered thoughts in readiness for worship, or are such words the focus or the medium for worship itself? Does it matter? I will (with Sikhs) repeat 'Satnam, Satnam' – the one reality whose name is truth…

Lotus

From words to pictures: the temple is full of pictures and religious symbols. These too I carry away in my memory for future reflection. Of all the water images that I encounter in Indian religious texts and iconography (of fords, rafts, boats across the ocean of existence) the lotus most often springs to mind.

Hindus' depictions of Lord Brahma, God as creator of the cosmos, show him seated on a lotus flower, with its stem growing from the navel of the sleeping Lord Vishnu, God as maintainer of all that is. Visitors to Hindu homes and temples are more likely to see vividly coloured pictures of Lakshmi, bestower of plenty, standing or seated upon a lotus. In some pictures elephants flank her, holding lotuses aloft in their upturned trunks. In these portrayals the opulent pink blooms convey divine bounty and beneficence.

But when spiritual masters bid us to be like the lotus, their insight concerns perfect detachment, being unsullied by the world, unswayed by desire. The loveliest of flowers is unstained by the mud in which it is rooted. Its petals do not touch even the surface of the pool, let alone the muck below. This can be understood as a straightforward illustration of detachment. But the further point is the necessity of the mire. Without it, and its nourishment, there can be no lotus. So the lotus leads me to ponder rootedness, stillness, detachment, bounty, growth – here is an image which I welcome.

Interacting images

During a Woodbrooke weekend for exploration of 'Quakers and Hindus' in 2001 a Woodbrooke artist in residence, Caroline Jariwala, shared her work with us. Immediately, as viewer, I responded to the brilliant, and brilliantly juxtaposed, colours.

The canvases called out to me through Caroline's vibrant patterning and arresting forms – particularly the thrust of sculpted female arms. We sensed movement, the movement of silk being folded ready for tucking into the top of a sari petticoat, the ceaseless dance of *gopis* around blue-skinned, yellow-clad, flute-playing Lord Krishna (see cover illustration).

Only later did I realise that in one painting the dancing woman's decorated sticks, upheld in the swirl of the dance, formed a cross, and that the swirling *gopis* in our cover illustration were (like Jesus's disciples) twelve in number. I realised that Caroline was expressing her truth simultaneously through Indian image and Christian symbol. Her paintings take me back to my reflection on *puja* and worship.

Isn't life like this, as we draw on our different sources, draw from our different wells of truth? I receive each day from God (or from the universe, if that is truer to my conceptualising of experience), and each day I offer the day back to God in prayer (or meditation, or a song...), and then go on receiving it back, blessed in a perpetual rhythm of receiving and giving. The day which I receive back is for sharing – and, if I trust, there will always be just enough to share. As I become conscious, through Caroline's painting, of the endless ebbing, flowing, gathering and dispersal, I think and visualise in Christian terms. The daily gift is in answer to my Christian prayer, 'Give us this day our daily bread'. I see the day as a cup, a chalice-shaped cup, that is received and offered and shared. At the same time, the rhythm of receiving, offering, receiving back and sharing is unmistakably a recurrent, ceaseless *puja*.

Interfaith worship?

Here I am not going to rehearse the discussions of what we mean by 'interreligious prayer' or by 'multifaith worship', and what – in the view of Christian writers from various denominations – is possible, desirable or theologically sound. (Broadly speaking those advocating 'interreligious prayer' assume that people of different faith communities can unite in a shared expression – for example using prayers that address 'God', but not 'Jesus', although deference to a Buddhist perspective may suggest alternatives to 'God' language also. 'Multifaith worship' would consist of distinctively Hindu, Muslim and other contributions, offered by members of the faiths in question.) Instead of covering this ground I can refer those who are interested in exploring this subject further to, on the one hand, compilations and anthologies (eg Cragg 1970; Potter and Braybrooke 1997; Braybrooke 2001) and, on the other hand, to analysis and argument.

The meticulous reasoning of the Catholic theologian, Gavin DCosta, for example, teases out distinctions between interreligious prayer which is 'cultic' (eg in a church's public act of worship) and interreligious prayer which is 'non-cultic' (as in spontaneous and private prayer) (2000). He mentions occasions for such experimentation that have arisen from friendships that span the boundaries between communities, as well as from crises that have drawn a religious response from people regardless of their religious affiliation. I think of prayers in Coventry cathedral's Chapel of Unity on World Aids Day and Hiroshima Day. We may be heartened by reading, after pages of DCosta's careful argument:

> I have been suggesting that plunging into the love of the triune God may well call us to risk finding an even greater love of God through interreligious prayer, and into discovering the darkness and mystery of God afresh. (2000: 166)

However, what I am proposing here is not that we embark on deliberate experiments with either interfaith or multifaith worship but rather that we recognise that our Meeting may already be an interfaith space. One sense in which Meeting for Worship is an interfaith space is the infinite capacity of its warm embracing silence. A Punjabi friend (from a Hindu cum Sikh background) feels comfortable in Meeting praying to her *pir* (the Muslim saint whom, like many Punjabis, she reveres). We do, however, need to be aware that the silence and lack of apparent activity can be every bit as offputting for a visitor of 'another faith' as it is for some Christians, as baffling as any (other) symbol.

When I suggest that Meeting is already an interfaith space this is also partly because 'other faiths' are accepted as springs for spoken ministry, even if 'other scriptures' are in most Meetings absent from the table. One Sunday I received the blessing of ministry from the Qur'an by a Friend who is also a Muslim. The previous week the surgeon had told me that I had breast cancer. I stood up to minister in Meeting as I felt moved to speak about temptation, about being tested and the need to live life experimentally. I said that I faced surgery and chemotherapy, but I did not mention breast cancer specifically. After a few minutes this Friend offered in spoken ministry the verse from the Qur'an which her son had that week selected for prayer time. It was called the Surah of the Expansion:

> In the name of Allah, most Gracious, most Merciful
> Have we not expanded thee thy breast?
> And removed from thee thy burden
> The which did gall thy back?
> And raised high the esteem in which thou art held?
> So, verily, with every difficulty there is relief:
> Verily, with every difficulty there is relief.
> Therefore, when thou art free from thine immediate task
> Still labour hard.
> And to thy Lord turn all thy attention.
> (Surah Al-Inshirah [no 94] as rendered in Ali 1946: 1755-1756)

Never had I felt so powerfully the unity between scripture,

ministry and my immediate need. I was glad that the scripture was the Qur'an.

So our Meetings are also interfaith in the sense that, as interfaith pilgrims, we ourselves bring to Meeting insights and questioning that draw on a range of reading and experience that crosses boundaries. It has been my experience that by being present at, say, Hindu *puja* not only do I start to take a fresh look at the religious practice of (other) Christians, but I bring more melodies, images and understandings into my own silent worship. Kim Knott has acknowledged that she brings to her spoken ministry in Meeting her particular gift of knowledge of other faiths, just as another Friend brings deep knowledge of the Bible (Nesbitt 1999a).

If we do wish to experiment, then the attentive reading of a book of prayers, meditations and words of hope, sensitively gathered from many traditions, may prepare us for Meeting and deepen our worship. I have mentioned Kenneth Cragg's *Alive to God* (1970). Marcus Braybrooke's *Learn to Pray* (2001) could bring fresh inspiration from many faiths to many Friends. Our Meetings may already be fostering, or come to foster, a spirituality which is at once deeply Quaker and profoundly interfaith – perhaps what Alan Race has called an 'interspirituality in waiting' (2001).

CHAPTER FIVE

What is Truth?

Trouthe is the hyeste thing that man may hope.
(Geoffrey Chaucer: *The Canterbury Tales*, The Frankleyn's Tale 1.75)

Love the truth more than all.
(George Fox: Epistle 65 in Ambler 2001: 16)

We might call such bedrock that interconnects all life
'the Body of Christ' or call it 'the Buddha nature,
Allah, Brahma, Jah, Tao and the Great Cosmic Mother'.
(McIntosh 2000: 166)

The words

In chapter three we concentrated on the lenses that are usually
invisible to us, and in chapter four I drew out some insights
from worship. These are two of the ways in which I have
approached truth. But I have postponed until this chapter a
headlong look at what we mean by truth. (For one sustained
and stimulating exploration of the history of truth try Felipe
Fernandez-Armesto's *Truth: A History and a Guide for the Perplexed*
[1997] in which he divides his subject into the truth that we
feel, the truth that we are told, the truth that we think out for

ourselves and the truth that we perceive through our senses.)

Truth is an old English word. Steadfastness and trust-worthiness are at the core of its meaning. Truth is faithfulness and loyalty: a true likeness is faithful to what it portrays; a truthful statement is honest and sincere. It is also reliable. My dictionary of etymology tumbles together truth, troth, trust (and both trusty and trustee), trow, tryst and truce as proba-bly related terms, conceptually overlapping. Our English 'truth' has grown up with, into or out of, a family of words that embraces commitment, confidence, stewardship, meeting and covenant. Truth, it appears, is itself not a far cry from rela-tionship.

Truth is a word which crops up over and over again in George Fox's writings and so, appropriately, *Truth of the Heart* is the title of Rex Ambler's anthology (2001). As John Punshon reminds us (1990: 32), for George Fox and his contemporary followers testifying to truth meant unequivocally testifying to the Christ-ian faith as understood by Friends. But what else can truth mean? What does it mean for us as Quakers in our multifaith society?

The *Oxford English Dictionary* gives a primary definition of truth as (1) 'character of being, or disposition to be, true to a person, principle, cause etc; faithfulness, loyalty, constancy, steadfast allegiance…truthfulness'. This is followed by (2) 'conformity with fact, agreement with reality, accuracy, correct-ness' and (3) 'something that is true…true religious belief or doctrine, orthodoxy'. I suggest that we free (1) from the con-strictions of (2) and (3) and that as pilgrims we do not let (3) overshadow the others. For example, our relations with Buddhists, Hindus or Muslims may benefit more from respect for their true-ness to their tradition than from debating with them whether there is a God or whether God is one and what this means.

From other languages the words which turn into 'truth' in their English translation carry their own wealths of meaning and association. In summary, Greek *aletheia* and Latin *veritas* are truth as the opposite of falseness and of mere appearance. ('Aletheia' will remind Philip Pullman's readers of the mysterious 'alethiometer'.) From Arabic *haqq* is translated as 'the true, the real, that which is exactly the opposite to *batil*, the unreal, the transitory' (Bowker 1997: 408). Al Haqq (the True) is one of God (Allah)'s titles.

From India the syllables *'sat'* and *'sach'* are translated as truth (see the Hindu and Sikh quotations on page 14). Many Friends will have reflected upon Gautama Buddha's Four Noble Truths – *satyani* in Sanskrit, *sachchani* in Pali. If you have Sikh friends you will notice that many Sikh forenames begin with the syllable *sat*, meaning truth. Indeed one popular name is Satnam, the word translated above as 'truth by name' (eg in the fourth of chapter one's opening quotations, describing the 'one reality'). *Sat* and *sach* are related to Sanskrit's *satya* which means truth in the sense of being, of reality, of what really is.

Importantly, recurrent in Indian thought is *satya*'s oneness, the unity behind apparent diversity. Many times I have heard a Hindu state that, according to the Veda, 'Truth is one but the wise know it by many names'. Despite some disturbing lapses, Hindus have, with this conviction, offered the world, over many centuries, an example of the reasonably peaceful co-existence of alternative interpretations of truth.

Together with this openness to diverse understandings of truth is a time-honoured acceptance of fundamental uncertainty, the classic agnosticism of the Rig Veda. Here we have a soliloquy from at least 1300 years before Jesus:

> Who can tell whence and how arose this universe?
> The gods are later than its beginning;
> Who knows therefore whence comes this creation?
> Only the One who sees in highest heaven.
> He only knows whence came the universe

And whether it was made or uncreated.
He only knows, or perhaps he knows not.
(Rig Veda: X 129, adapted from the translation in Mascaro 1965: 10)

Truth claims

By contrast with this ancient, apparently untroubled tentative-ness, and with India's sense of truth/*satya* as ultimate reality, in the west truth has often come down to propositions. Many of us today puzzle intellectually, and agonise existentially, over religious statements of truth which are exclusive truth claims. We can identify as our cultural bedrock the exclusiveness of Hebrew – and subsequently of Christian – proclamation. Take for example Jehovah's mountain-top diktat: 'You shall have no other gods before me' (Exodus 20.3) and the fulminations of the psalmist and prophets against the heathen who have gone after other gods. (By capitalising 'God' and giving 'gods' lower case our linguistic heritage embodies such certainties.) Or take: 'No-one comes to the Father, but by me' (John 14.6). This bedrock has supported the creeds of Christendom – and so, too, the cruelty of Crusaders and of the Inquisition.

Our longing for firm, unconditional truth is of a piece with the pre-Socratic philosophers' quest 2500 years ago for a single underlying element (air, water or fire). This quest marks the beginnings of centuries of European science and rational-ism and is part of Christianity's plural inheritance. Steeped in this philosophical tradition too we readily agree 'If this is true, that cannot be true.' Both cannot be the case.

In the area of the dictionary definition (3) above, ie of truth as religions and ideologies, we are rightly wary of relaxing our guard against intellectual sloppiness and mental muddle. How can we accept as equal and interchangeable the Islamic profession of faith, to which we turn shortly, and 'No-one comes to the Father, but by me'? (I will return to this verse in chapter six.)

As Quakers part of our unease with truth claims draws upon a temperamental and a historical resistance to creeds:

> We do not in the least deprecate the attempt...to formulate intellectually the ideas which are implicit in religious experience...But it should always be recognised that all such attempts are provisional, and can never be assumed to possess the finality of ultimate truth.
> (*Quaker faith & practice* 1995: 27.23)

Creeds?

Sometimes faiths are called creeds. To make this equation is to assume that, like Christianity, other faiths, too, have at their centre a statement of required belief which is uniquely true, and that this doctrinal dimension is more important than the others. Certainly Muslims profess their faith uncompromisingly in the words of the Shahada, the fundamental 'pillar' of Islam: 'La ilah illa Allah wa-Muhammad arRasul Allah' ie '(I bear witness that) there is no God but God and Muhammad is the messenger of God'. Pronouncing this is the only formal requirement for entry into the Muslim community. Nonetheless many Muslims would point out firmly that Islam is not a 'creed' but a way of life.

Despite debate on who is and who is not a Jew, to be Jewish depends basically not on assent to a creed but on being born to a Jewish mother (except in the case of converts). For many, being Jewish means maintaining *kashrut* (food purity, involving a kosher kitchen etc), rather than making public avowals of faith. This having been said, the Jewish liturgy includes the Shema, a declaration of God's unity, which begins (from Deuteronomy 6.4-9):

> Hear, O Israel: the Lord our God is one Lord; and
> you shall love the Lord your God with all your heart,
> and with all your soul, and with all your might.

Hindus too are (for the most part) Hindu by birth and culture, although in some settings (in Bali and Trinidad, for instance) Hindu statements of faith are set out. These spell out that God is one, that the law of *karma* (moral cause and effect) operates, and that souls are reincarnated until they attain *moksha* (liberation from successive rebirths). But affirming such statements (which may well be more evident outside India) is not a prerequisite for being Hindu, which is usually a matter of being born into a Hindu family. For many ordinary Hindus in India the concern is more likely to be with individual deities (while maintaining an abiding sense of a higher impersonal reality) than with 'one God' as understood by Christians, Jews and Muslims.

Buddhist teaching is more clearly grounded in a set of principles, which the Buddha articulated in the first sermon that he gave – in the deer park at Sarnath in north India – soon after his enlightenment. In this sermon he set out the four noble truths. (1) *Dukkha* (which means transience or suffering) is universal. (2) It is the thirst for satisfaction from what passes away which causes suffering. Yet (3) *dukkha* can be brought to an end if we cease to fuel the fires of greed, hatred and ignorance, and so attain nirvana. (4) The summary of ways to do this is the 'eightfold path' to enlightenment, a path which includes right speech and right mindfulness. But is this a 'creed'?

The Sikhs' *mul mantar* (literally 'root formula') opens the scriptures, and is recited five times by candidates during the rite of initiation with holy water which is known as the *amrit sanskar*. Devout Sikhs daily recite in the sacred language of their scripture:

> There is One Being
> Truth by Name
> Primal Creator
> Without fear
> Without enmity
> Timeless in form

Unborn
Self-existent
The grace of the Guru.
(as translated in Singh 1995: 47)

But, unlike Christian creeds, this formula has never been used as a test of orthodoxy. We may decide that in some way these formulations from different faiths seek to encapsulate truth, even though not all are 'creeds' in the Christian sense. We may see an attempt to compare them as useful for our quest to find out what truth is.

Oneness and uniqueness

If so, we soon bump into the number one (in eg 'The Lord is one'), and we are confronted by the meaning of oneness and of uniqueness. The human quest for truth expresses itself over and over again in terms of 'one'. A key dilemma opens up when we examine Sikhs' *'ik oan kar'* (There is one God? One reality is?) Should we understand it as paralleling Jewish, Christian and Muslim monotheism, or as echoing the 8th century CE Hindu philosopher Shankara?

For Shankara there is only one reality. Any appearances of differentiation eg between God and creation are actually an illusion. They are ignorance which can be dispelled by realising that there is only one reality (*brahman*). When we see things as being fundamentally different from each other we are as deluded as the person who treads on a rope and springs back, thinking that it is a deadly cobra. This philosophical understanding of oneness is known as *advaita* in Sanskrit, that is non-dualism or monism. Similarly Zen Buddhist teachers explain that 'the truth to be realised is that there is only the Buddha-nature underlying all appearance'.

For Zoroastrians, Jews, Christians and Muslims, on the other hand, 'one' is used to describe God, so making the point that other gods are false – they are worshipped in error. In this understanding God is other than the world (which he created), and he is also other than evil or the Evil One, the devil (who figures less prominently in Jewish belief than in Zoroastrian, Christian and Muslim belief).

In Christian formulations of belief 'one' is stressed. We have only to listen to the Nicene creed: 'We believe in one God. We believe in one Lord, Jesus Christ, the only son of God…of one Being with the Father…We believe in one holy, catholic and apostolic Church. We acknowledge one baptism for the forgiveness of sins.'

What does it mean to be one? When Jesus said 'I and the Father are one' (John 10.30) was this a unitary oneness or the at one-ness of being in perfect harmony? We can reflect on whether one always = single, singular, indivisible, or whether it can be complex and multiple. (Christian understanding of God as a trinity, as triune, illustrates this second possibility.)

I suggest that rather than agonising or debating the mutual exclusiveness of human formulations of oneness we dwell upon the oneness of harmony and union, the inclusiveness of different aspects. For this we will all find images that are helpful – the light being broken into a rainbow of colours as it passes through the prism is a Quaker favourite, lovingly embroidered into a panel of the Quaker tapestry displayed in Kendal Meeting House. And here are the images offered by Chief Rabbi Jonathan Sacks:

> There are multiple universes of faith, each capturing something of the radiance of being and refracting it into the lives of its followers, none refuting or excluding the others, each as it were the native language of its followers, but combining in a hymn of glory to the creator. (2002: 204)

In seeking to reconcile apparently different truths we can learn from the Jains. Jains are one of the smallest faith communities – with probably no more than 8 million worldwide and fewer than 30,000 in the UK (mostly in London and Leicester). Their practical, humble, accepting approach to seeming diversities of truth is summed up in the word *anekantavada*. This is variously translated as the many-pointedness, non-one-sidedness or many-sidedness of reality, as non-absolutism and no one single viewpoint. 'Different people think about different aspects of the same reality, and therefore their partial findings are contradictory to one another.' (www.jaintirths.com).

Can apparently incompatible expressions of truth be regarded as facets of truth? That old Indian image of the elephant surrounded by perplexed blind men reappears. The man feeling around the trunk is sure that the elephant is like a snake, the person investigating its legs knows that elephants are like tree trunks. The most adventurous, who has reached an ear, knows that elephants are like winnowing baskets.

Such an image for human attempts at knowing what really is helps us to understand how truth can take so many guises. But it does not help us to discern the truth which we have an existential need to affirm in the mounting bewilderment and dislocation of survival.

Convergence and divergence

We may adopt the line that we will set to one side apparently competing 'creeds', and incompatible understandings of God or the universe, and focus instead upon convergences between the teachings of different faiths. Truth may lie this way. Perhaps this was what the Muslim Indian emperor Akbar had in mind when he said, 'I try to take good from all opinion with the sole object of ascertaining the truth' (Bowker 1997: 37). We note that certain themes recur: love and compassion, and life after death soon come to mind. But for every convergence there is also a divergence. Divine incarnation features in both Hindu and Christian belief – but Christians' insistence on the uniqueness of God's incarnation in Jesus of Nazareth is nonsensical to Hindus who know that Lord Vishnu takes human form at different junctures when *dharma* (righteousness) is under threat. Death is not the end of life (so our different faiths agree), but Muslim and Christian teaching on heaven and hell differ from each other and are at variance with Hindu acceptance that the cycle of birth and death continues over many lifetimes. Time itself is a linear dimension for the Semitic faiths, but cyclical for Hindu and related faiths.

Nonetheless we may, as interfaith pilgrims, hearken to some of the resonances between faith traditions, and ponder whether these are inklings of truth. One resonance between traditions is emphasis on the need for detachment from the fruits of our actions (ie doing what we know to be right, without hoping for a reward). It means shedding desire, lust and greed: here we have a continuum which Buddhists, Christians, Hindus, Sikhs and others acknowledge, albeit in different terms. Another example of convergence is the image of the passionate love of the bride for her husband/lover. This features in the Sikh scriptures and in the Christian experience and exposition of the Cistercian abbot, Bernard of Clairvaux (1090-1153), of John of the Cross (1542-1591) and of so many other Christian mystics (Hick 1999: 149-150). For Hindus the soul's passionate desire for God is expressed by Radha's and her cow-girl companions' longing for Krishna (see the cover of this book) as they dance to the notes of his flute and are united with him.

As Quakers we may find ourselves listening to the sound of silence in the context of different faiths – and noting resemblances between the breathing and silent intoning of the Jesus prayer by Greek Orthodox monks on Mount Athos, and the spiritual discipline of Hindus' *prana* (breath) yoga and of Buddhist meditation. The sound of silence...and so on to paradox.

Paradox

> He moves, and he moves not. He is far, and he is near.
> He is within all, and he is outside all.
> (Isa Upanishad 5 in Mascaro 1965: 49)

Along with this approach of welcoming convergences and common ground I want to emphasise the importance of embracing paradox (as in the ancient Hindu text above). Zen Buddhist teachers deliberately present us with apparent contradictions (or 'koans'), and so shift our perceptions of how things are. 'What is the sound of one hand clapping?' is a 'koan': it takes us beyond our intellects (Braybrooke 2001: 30). Other faith traditions too contain paradox – the 'unstruck music' in Guru Nanak's poem in chapter four is an instance – and these paradoxes may offer us a way of apprehending that truth is inapprehensible in its entirety.

Detachment and involvement provide a spiritual conundrum for the Indic faiths. The classical Hindu resolution to this was to allocate successive periods of the human lifespan to involvement in family life (*grihastha*), to *vanaprastha* (withdrawal into the jungle to concentrate on spiritual matters), and finally *sannyasa* (renunciation of everything including one's name). The Sikh Gurus' response was to urge Sikhs to practise a simultaneous involvement in worldly affairs and centredness on the *nam*, the divine reality. In early Gurus' terms this meant constant *nam japan* (repeating of God's name) and *seva* (voluntarily serving others). In the language of later Gurus the paradox was encapsulated as *sant sipahi*, the saint soldier, who is spiritually focused whilst remaining alert and equipped for action. Chapter six will pick up the theme of being a saint soldier.

The Christian tradition recurrently poses the dilemma of how to reconcile faith and reason. In the gospel Jesus announces 'If anyone would be first, he must be last of all and servant of all' (Mark 9. 35) and, in no less paradoxical mode, St Paul experiences 'the Lord' telling him: 'My power is made perfect in weakness' (2 Corinthians 12.9). Christian doctrine affirms Jesus' full humanity and his full divinity. The Danish philosopher Søren Kierkegaard called this the Absolute Paradox.

Experientially we can come to a deep affirmation of the paradoxical claims made by St Francis of Assisi: 'It is in giving that we receive; it is in losing that we find.' Once we own these affirmations we are emboldened to continue: 'It is in dying that we are born to everlasting life.' I was fortunate as a schoolgirl that for our morning assemblies *Songs of Praise* provided our hymns. Through repeatedly singing these lines I internalised Francis Thompson's startling paradoxes:

> O world invisible, we view thee,
> O world intangible, we touch thee,
> O world unknowable, we know thee,
> Inapprehensible, we clutch thee.
> (*The Kingdom of God*)

This positive valuing of paradox within our own tradition can enable us to be open to the possibility that what appears irreconcilably contrary to our own truth or tradition may be another aspect of a greater truth. As I have suggested in chapter two, Quakers have a substantial tradition of singling out from, say, Hindu writing verses that affirm their own instincts about life's purpose. But in our theological explorations we must not fear or avoid what seems to deny or overthrow our own truth. If we can hold biblical paradoxes and seemingly incompatible Jewish/Christian truths in a creative tension, so too I suggest we can savour sentiment or conviction in the scripture or preaching of Muslims or Buddhists, knowing that this way, however obscurely, may lie a greater wholeness, even though the surface truth they convey is initially incompatible with our own take on truth.

We may be able to take particular (if vast) paradoxes from our own tradition and find in them clues for holding together the contradictory pulls of different communities' insights. The Christians' understanding of God as a Trinity of Persons provides one such example. The emphasis on unity affords a basis for shared exploration with Jews and Muslims; the understanding of relationality and persons in the plural (father, son and spirit) eases our respectful entry into Hindu or Pagan valuing of manifold divinity.

Parker Palmer, the American Quaker educationist, has written persuasively of the need to 'think the world together' instead of perpetuating a 'culture of disconnection' that values analysing and so polarising (1998). If we add to the 'either/or' discipline of scientific thinking the Hebrew prophets' resounding condemnations of other gods, we start to recognise the reasons why living with truths that seem mutually exclusive (eg God as one and God as many) may disturb us. But let us for a while at least concur with Palmer that 'when a person is healthy and whole, the head and the heart are both-and, not either-or'.

In conclusion

In every part of this chapter truth emerges elusively, triumphantly multi-faceted. This is so, whether we look at the meanings of the words which translate as 'truth', or at the seeming contradictions (as well as convergences and overlaps) between and within traditions and their revered writings. In suggesting that we value paradox, and affirm our capacity to 'think the world together', I am offering one approach to discerning truth in a bewildering world. A glance at the family of words to which 'truth' belongs reminds us to value what emerges in relationships of trust, and what manifests in steadfast integrity. We must not get stuck in abstractions.

We have seen that another approach to discerning what is true is to try to work out how truths relate to one another – truths which are enshrined in different scriptures, then internalised and articulated by different faith communities. However, rather than aiming to arrive at or distil a core of shared or overlapping truths, my suggestion is that we explore truth as something that emerges especially in our encounters with others. In other words, truth itself is essentially relational and dynamic. For, to half-echo an earlier Swarthmore lecturer, Sydney Bailey, truth is – like peace – a process (Bailey 1993). Truth is not discovered in isolation from others. Even apparently solitary mystics think in ways which refer to the thoughts of others, and any revelation of truth can only be understood and communicated in ways which involve language, that most social of human attributes. So, truths can 'talk to each other' (in the words of the Swarthmore Lecture Committee's invitation to me to write this book), but they do so in the sense that truth is itself dialogical. Truth is already 'interfaith': it is in our own inner conversations and in our exchanges with others that we catch sight of truth. To engage with truth we must tune into this conversation within ourselves and between individuals of faith in different communities.

Before we move on to the final chapter, with its emphasis on engagement, steadfastness and integrity, we do well to listen to the Muslim, Farid Esack's, conviction, forged in his struggle against apartheid in South Africa:

> People with a religious commitment may choose to believe that truth is exclusively an eternal and pre-existing reality beyond history. However, people also make truth.
> (1997: 10)

And we should listen again to George Fox who spoke of living in the truth and dwelling in the truth. For example:

> Take heed of knowledge, for it puffeth up, but dwell in the truth, and be what ye speak.
>
> (Epistle 58 in Ambler 2001: 82)

CHAPTER SIX

Betruthal

Truth is then neither a philosophical notion nor a matter of ethical principles – even ones as worthy as the Quaker testimonies. Such codifying of behaviour is actually the very opposite of the experience to which Quakerism points us, which is obedient to something alive and dependable within, a source of revelation available to all beyond any system of religious belief.
(Wildwood 1999: 83)

'Plight' means to promise or pledge, and 'troth' is an old word for truth and trust. In the Bible, truth implies active commitment; as in 'will you be true to me?'
(Adams 2000: 13)

Highest is Truth: higher still is truthful living.
(Adi Granth: Rag Sri 62)

The gist of my final chapter lies in these three quotations – two by contemporary Quakers and the third translated from the words of Guru Nanak (see: www.answersoflife.com/philosophy/sikhism/beliefs.htm or www.sikhs.org/philos.htm). His words carry us forward from Geoffrey Chaucer's frankleyn (quoted at the top of chapter five): they propel us from abstraction to action, from philosophy to fidelity.

In previous chapters we have acknowledged the intellectual dilemma that is posed by apparently incompatible, or at least non-identical, truth claims and we have considered the potential value of paradox. We have looked too at the value of examining assumptions that are embedded in the way that we use terms such as 'faith', 'other faiths' and 'interfaith'. We have seen the ways in which a reflective embrace of image and metaphor can free us up and enrich us. We have admitted to carrying cultural baggage and have tried on, and taken off, a few conceptual lenses. But this is armchair stuff...

Temperament will determine whether we are more eager to think with philosophical clarity or to act out our insights in changing society. This said, as Quakers we are already caught up in an experiential approach to truth. This requires us to test and experiment, to develop our capacity to discern what is true, and to express this faithfully in action.

After reflecting on how, in our plural world, we can discern truth this chapter looks at engagement with truth through the metaphor of 'a turning towards', then through the act of betruthal/ betrothal and we will consider Mahatma Gandhi's *satyagraha* (getting a grip on truth). Love, faithfulness and struggle are recurrent themes for us as interfaith pilgrims. This struggle means that we will have the experience of being tested as well as putting to the test.

Tasting and testing

Discernment may at first suggest images of seeing (as when Muslims know that it is time for the daily Ramadan fast to begin because there is enough light to distinguish a white thread from a black one). In speaking of God as light John Punshon suggests that 'perhaps the most important feature of the light metaphor is that light is the medium of discernment' (1990: 69). But it is the sense of taste, rather than sight, which is evoked in many metaphors. In fact a Hindu image of *viveka* (discrimination, discernment) is the swan, mythically talented in separating milk from water with its bill. Tasting may mean for us 'mystical' experiences of inexplicable calm or bliss or of total oneness with nature.

In Jewish scripture Psalm 34. 8 invites us to 'taste and see that the Lord is good'. Amongst the guidance for Friends on living with diversity are the following words of Marjorie Sykes:

> Every tree is to be known by its fruits: not by its deadwood or thorns or parasites, but by the fruit of its own inner life and nature. We all know the fruits of the Spirit and recognise the beauty of holiness in our own ancestral tree...the flowers of unselfish living may be found growing in other people's gardens and...rich fruits of the Spirit may be tasted from other people's trees. They spring from the same Holy Spirit of Truth, the same Seed of God, whose power moves us through Christ.
> (Marjorie Sykes, *Quaker faith & practice*, 1995: 27.11)

Here Marjorie is picking up Jesus' guideline for distinguishing a true prophet from a false one (Matthew 7.15-20; Luke 6.43-44). St Paul named the 'fruits of the spirit' as 'love, peace, patience, kindness, goodness, faithfulness, gentleness, self-control (Galatians 5.22-23).

We may be less at ease with traditional Christian expressions of faith, but this metaphor of fruits conveys the soundest basis that we know for recognising the truth at work in the lives of our neighbours. For John Hick, philosopher-theologian, it is the spiritual and moral fruits evident in the lives of people of all faiths which make exclusive claims for the superiority of any one faith untenable (see eg Hick 1990: 17; 1995: 13-16). In his assessment there is no good reason to believe that any one of the great religious traditions has shown itself to be more productive of love/compassion than any other.

Of course, this metaphor of fruit does suggest that it will not only be the sweetness, the attractiveness of something which is an indication of its truth, but also its potential for nourishing and sustaining us. Do you remember the reference in chapter two to the number of disparaging comments about contemporary 'pick and mix' spirituality? As John Hull's *Mishmash* (1991) discussed so acutely, critics of a multifaith religious education syllabus resorted to rhetorical comparison with unwholesome or unsavoury cuisine. Instinctively people turn to the language of flavour, satisfaction and nutrition. We say that the proof of the pudding is in the eating.

But all this talk of fruit and tasting does not necessarily help us to decide between the competing truth claims on which believers may claim to base their selfless service of neighbour. Keith Ward reminds us that by agreeing to John Hick's argument we are not saying that all paths 'are the same, or that they are equally direct and sure' (Ward 2000: 69). We may also consider whether (given that people are in so many cases spiritually plural, multiply influenced people, and that many profess no faith or reject religion as they know it) it is valid for us to be regarding an individual's behaviour as the 'fruits' of a single faith tradition, which we then judge on this basis. (Into my mind's eye comes a Sikh friend, with an enquiring mind, who grew up among Hindus and Muslims and attended a Roman Catholic school. Are his evident kindness and wisdom a measure only of the Sikh faith?)

In any case truth has to be wider, less static than any truth claims. Spiritual fruits are more likely to grow from truth in the *Oxford English Dictionary*'s sense of (1) 'steadfast allegiance' than from truth as (3) 'religious orthodoxy'. So (as I argued in a radio interview about gurus), devotion to a spiritual teacher, even one whom others discern to be in some sense 'false', can be seen to inspire selfless joy and service in many dedicated followers. I suggest, therefore, that rather than using such fruits as evidence of the truth of a teaching – or for that matter of the teacher's divine nature, or even of his/her human probity – we draw inspiration from the spirituality of many committed disciples.

In responding to this steadfastness and examining religious teachings we need to exercise discernment. An image from India springs to mind. The mediaeval Indian *bhakti* (mystical/devotional) poet Kabir uses the image of the ant and the elephant, and this lit up my reflection on discernment. God 'is like sugar spilled in the sand that an elephant cannot pick up' (Vaudeville 1974: 331). We should become like ants, Kabir says, separating the sugar from the sand and eating it. We do not need to be weighty Friends, people of stature or intellectual clout in order to taste, absorb and draw strength from truth. This, Kabir's image suggests, is possible, and may well be only possible, if we remain not only grounded but also low key and unpretentious.

Our metaphor of tasting is one way of expressing the fact that recognising what is true requires us to put our insights to the test, to experiment with truth. When Damaris Parker Rhodes spoke of her 'serious experiment with truth' (see page 27) she echoed the title of Mahatma Gandhi's autobiography (1927). For Gandhi 'there is no other God than Truth', and the seeker's total commitment to the way of nonviolent action (*ahimsa*) is crucial. Testing means action.

> But this much I can say with assurance, as a result of all my experiments, that a perfect vision of Truth can only follow a complete realization of Ahimsa.
> (1927: 420)

Whether or not we prioritise *ahimsa*, experimenting with

truth means putting principle into practice, it means total dedication to action. It is not a cerebral pursuit but physical and practical, realising and activating an ideal.

On the wall of the room in Woodbrooke in which Gandhi stayed in 1931 hangs a framed copy of 'Gandhiji's talisman' ('Gandhiji' is the usual, respectful way in which speakers of Indian languages refer to him):

> Whenever you are in doubt or when Self becomes too much with you, apply the following test: Recall the face of the poorest and the weakest man whom you may have seen and ask yourself if the step you contemplate is going to be of any use to him.

In the spirit of science's experimental tradition we may decide to put to the test, in our own lives, principles – such as nonviolence – which others have tested so rigorously.

Within the Society of Friends, too, we have proven help in discerning the way forward in personal dilemmas. Patricia Loring has examined discernment with particular clarity as the practice of 'an on-going intentional openness and prayerful attentiveness to intimations of divine presence and guidance' (1992: 3). This approach applies to discerning religious insights and truth claims as well as to resolving personal dilemmas. She underlines how important our Quaker community is as a 'test or touchstone for authenticated leadings' (1992: 7) together with testing against the 'Bible or with the writings of spiritual leaders or saintly people from Quaker and other traditions' (1992: 8).

The practice of silence also facilitates discernment. Silence and stillness...do we practise these throughout the week? This stillness is our strength enabling us to remain faithful when we ourselves are tested in the course of our pilgrimage. In reflecting on discernment John Punshon stressed fidelity – long term faithfulness – together with perseverance and the love of truth as 'the guarantee of spiritual discernment' (1990).

Being tested

It is often through dilemmas that we feel ourselves put to the test. This experience is as much a part of our ongoing discernment of truth as any testing and experiment that we set up. The stories of our predecessors on the path of spiritual pilgrimage suggest that as we test for truth so too our commitment to truth will be tested. We may experience this in physical suffering, in depression, or in terms of Jesus' 'temptation' in the wilderness by the Devil (Luke 4.1-13). (There is a less well-known account of how Kalyug, the spirit of the present troubled age, tempted Guru Nanak with 'a palace studded with pearls, a world encrusted with diamonds and command over all lands' [McLeod 1980: 45-49].) We may be tested by illness, bereavement and other overwhelming circumstances. We may pray in Jesus' words 'Lead us not into temptation' (Luke 11.4) or 'Father, if thou art willing, remove this cup of suffering from me' (Luke 22.42). Whether our assurance of what is true dissolves, or whether a certainty of truth upholds us, the experience of being tested and the sense of testing are inextricably related.

In Jewish scripture Job stands for all who feel themselves tried to the uttermost by God. Through an apparently relentless onslaught of adversity may come an awareness of truth which goes far beyond any merely intellectual proposition. This awareness may be wonder at ineffable mystery, or it may be a deep assurance. Our experience of being tested may be one of struggling. Also from Jewish tradition comes Jacob, wrestling with the man/angel/God, and coming away both wounded and blessed (Genesis 32.22-32). In our tussle with the angel all truths – all truth claims – may evaporate, leaving over time a deeper certainty, a truth. This may or may not find ready expression in words, even to ourselves. Emily Brontë's cry 'no coward soul is mine' suggests some turbulence of spirit through which her certainty shone that:

> Vain are the thousand creeds
> That move men's hearts: unutterably vain:
> Worthless as withered weeds,
> Or idlest froth amid the boundless main.
>
> . . . .
>
> Though earth and moon were gone,
> And suns and universes ceased to be,
> And Thou wert left alone,
> Every existence would exist in Thee.
>
> ('Last Lines')

Whatever remains with us from the struggle will be our truth.

Turning and facing

We are also quite likely to recall points in our lives when we changed direction or felt that we were being guided. Turning and facing are metaphors for our spiritual engagement with truth which appear in many writings. If we turn away we do not comprehend:

> Turn but a stone, and start a wing!
> Tis ye, 'tis your estranged faces,
> That miss the many-splendoured thing.
>
> (Francis Thompson, The Kingdom of God)

To move from men and angels to the garden: sunflowers have faces that remind us of the sun and as they also face towards the sun their name is doubly appropriate. This double entendre vividly reminds us that the orientation of our lives, what we become and how we appear to others are part and parcel of each other. In Guru Nanak's teaching turning, or rather facing, is vital for the individual seeking to escape self-centredness and associated blocks to spiritual progress. But what is needed is

for us to be *gurmukh*, to be facing unwaveringly towards the
Guru, towards the giver of enlightenment. Or to quote St
Paul's words: 'And we all, with unveiled face, beholding the
glory of the Lord, are being changed into his likeness from one
degree of glory to another' (2 Corinthians 3.18).

Similarly, George Fox exhorted his hearers and readers to 'turn
to the light', the light that was Christ, or which was at least 'from
Christ' (Punshon 2001: 48-50). In each individual who turns
towards it the light acts redemptively. The theologian, David
Ford, has explored the concept of 'facing' – and in particular the
concept of 'facing Jesus Christ' – in his book, *Self and Salvation*.

> Christianity is characterised by the simplicity and
> complexity of facing: being faced by God, embodied
> in the face of Christ; turning to face Jesus Christ in
> faith; being members of a community of the face:
> seeing the face of God reflected in creation and espe-
> cially in each human face, with all the faces in our
> heart related to the presence of the face of Christ.
> (1999: 24-25)

Facing is a Muslim emphasis too. Surah (verse) 10.105 of
the Qur'an bids the reader 'set thy face towards religion with
true piety'. In a literal sense, whenever a Muslim carries out the
prescribed daily prayers ('reads' *namaz*), she or he faces towards the
kaba at Makkah, as shown by the *mihrab* (niche) in any mosque.

In one of my seminars this year a Muslim student showed
the rest of us her compass, a dial which indicates for her the
direction of Makkah, while the needle points north. No
compass needle actually reaches what it is pointing towards.
But compass needles are reliable and help us find our way. They
also remind us that, while the north that is marked on our maps
is unchanging, north itself, the magnetic field, is shifting,
elusive. When we have turned our gaze, redirected our whole

being, we are ready to engage with truth. Through engaging we may find ourselves realigned at deeper and deeper levels.

Satyagraha

For this engagement with truth and commitment to truth Gandhi (the Mahatma or great self) has provided a word: *satyagraha*, a compound of the word 'satya' which you met in chapter five. This was Gandhi's chosen name for his campaign of nonviolent non-cooperation. Later, Gandhi himself came to distinguish 'non-cooperation and civil resistance' from *satyagraha* itself as the 'offshoots' of *satyagraha* (Patel 1988: 51). *Satyagraha* bears the meaning of nonviolent resistance because of the particular means that Gandhi identified and implemented for overthrowing two particular wrongs: the oppression of Indians in South Africa and the subjugation of Indians in India by the British Raj. But in recognition of *satya*'s meaning as truth, the English rendering 'truth force' also appears for *satyagraha*. Gandhi explained his choice of name for the movement as 'the Force which is born of Truth and Love or non-violence' (1928: 173).

Other ways in which the Sanskrit word *graha* can accurately be translated are 'seizing' and 'holding firmly'. So we could validly translate *satyagraha* as '(conflict resolution by) holding on to truth'. Certainly, however Gandhi himself chose to translate the word that he had compounded, he practised *satyagraha* in this sense of seizing and holding firmly on to truth too.

Our own grasping of truth, our personal *satyagraha*, may issue in very different action from Gandhi's, depending upon the injustice or other need that speaks to us. For most of us our *satyagraha* will not mean starting a new mass movement, inspiring hundreds of millions of people and making global history. Our *satyagraha* may be an individual dedication – or re-dedication – to writing letters to prisoners or to Members of Parliament or to heads of government. It may be our response to asylum seekers,

to environmental polluters or drug users. It may be our commitment to give to our neighbours – and to receive from them.

To use a Sikh image, I suggest we all become *sant-sipahi*,
saint-soldiers, contemplatives ready to spring into action on
behalf of others. Soldiers? This means turning, facing – and
more. In the Hindus' *Bhagavad Gita* we have Lord Krishna's
exhortation to the shrinking Arjuna on the brink of battle
against close relatives. In some sense we must fight rather than
withdraw in sensitive and principled inaction. (As Friends do
we still only listen for the truth in the images that appeal to
us?) Our 'fight' may take the form of a concerted disciplined
'campaign' of drawing attention to a particular injustice and to
ways of restoring justice. Or our fight may involve a vigorous
reassessment of our resources of personality, experience and
potential. And to be a spiritual warrior may be, as Christina
Feldman has written, not 'seeking war but questing for truth'
(1994: 7).

All this comes close to what we mean by our Quaker testimony to truth. To quote my Swarthmore predecessor, John
Punshon, again:

> So the testimony of truth is not the discovery and
> application of principles, but the public side of private
> spiritual discernment. Here we encounter the coming
> together of mystical and prophetic experience, two
> modes of response to one reality.
> (1990: 68).

Betruthal

Engagement – not military engagement but the engagement of
two lovers – is how I picture our relationship with truth, a
truth that we are coming to know the more deeply we commit
ourselves to it. Hence 'betruthal', with its key aspects of love
and faithfulness.

As mentioned in chapter five, the love of lover for beloved, of wife for husband, of the soul for the Lord pervades the writing of the Christian saints Bernard of Clairvaux and Thérèse of Lisieux, and it also pervades Sikh scripture and Sufi writing. In spirit, the Gurus are saying, we long for this divine reality with the yearning of a bride parted from her husband. As the cover of this book reminds us, the human soul (like Krishna's cow-girl companions) is in love with God (here Lord Krishna). Each of us faces towards this divine love as we dance.

Our engagement with truth is a love affair which expresses itself in our love for neighbour and love for creation, in both passion and compassion. Insightfully writing of commitment to Christ, the American scholar, Diana Eck, reminds us that:

> The language of faith is the language of affection, of affirmation and commitment...and the language of faith is the language of love, not of judgement.
> (1993: 95)

Our own 'betruthal' is not a denial of the commitment of our neighbours, the uniqueness of our truth is not in opposition to their experiences of love and affirmation.

Betrothal, the commitment made prior to marriage, marks a serious intention of faithfulness in an exclusive lifelong relationship. We endeavour to be steadfast in our relationship with the truth, which we are constantly seeking, glimpsing and mediating in our interactions with our neighbours. On the steadfastness of our love for truth depends our spiritual discernment (Punshon 1990: 72). Our constancy to truth is open to, and inclusive of, others' glimpses and formulations of truth.

I have chosen the metaphor of betrothal deliberately in the knowledge of a recurrent image in Jewish/Christian tradition of association with other faiths as faithless adultery. The question: 'Is interreligious prayer like marital infidelity?' is part of the

Catholic theologian, Gavin DCosta's, title for the penetrating discussion of the possibility of interfaith prayer with which he concludes his study of *The Meeting of Religions and the Trinity* (2000). DCosta's metaphor echoes the prophet Hosea (in the 8th century BCE), pleading with the people of Israel who have been 'unfaithful' and deserted the one true God.

What better reminder of my own (and of the Society of Friends') Judaeo-Christian family of faith? For many Friends, and not only in the more evangelical meetings of the Americas, faithfulness to the Society's Christian calling is an issue. To this our response as interfaith pilgrims has to be one of soul-searching choice, and a faithfulness to an overwhelming sense that we too have a calling – to be bridges rather than pillars, let alone salespeople. So I will dwell quietly on the verse 'I am the way, the truth and the life. No-one comes to the Father, but by me' (John 14.6). I will reflect thankfully on Diana Eck's wise exposition (1993: 94) in which she points out that, in these words, Jesus was not pronouncing on the destiny of Hindus or Muslims. He was offering pastoral words of reassurance to an anxious follower on their last evening together.

These words, reported in the context of Jesus' imminent betrayal and death, can be heard as an exhortation to self-giving love. It is, I suggest, sacrificial love that is the gateway to truth. This may be through caring for others or for another. It is (in Buddhist terms) the way of *metta*, of loving compassion, for all creation. It is not the suicidal sacrifice which destroys others too for a cause. The face of the one whom we love most may be our inspiration. Mother Teresa saw Christ in every dying destitute who came for her help. Guru Gobind Singh's follower, the water-carrier Bhai Ghahnaiya, saw the face of his Guru in the fallen of both sides to whom he offered water from his leather water bag.

My faithfulness will be to the insight that my understanding of 'God' (and of truth) is reduced, impoverished, if I close my mind to my neighbours' experiences of duty, devotion and divinity. I will take the risk of living out a calling which so many people of integrity share. Expressed in theistic terms this is the awareness that 'Today, God wills to work through the dialogue and cooperation between many peoples of many faiths and non-faiths...' (Gwyn 1989-1997: 47).

With its resonances of loving faithfulness, 'betruthal' is a life-long commitment to 'the hyeste thing that man may hope', to living truth, and to love. It is both trust and faithfulness which constitute 'truthful living'. This is what I mean by 'betruthal'.

We remember, too, that betrothal has, in different societies, involved greater or lesser degrees of individual choice. Our being Quaker, too, has probably already involved choice in a way that being Jewish or Hindu often do not. So, too, our engagement with truth in a cross-cultural, interfaith way can be (or become) a conscious step.

Finally

Woodbrooke, the setting for interfaith explorations of recent years, is the uniquely supportive home in which I am drawing together the threads spun in earlier chapters. In my room here – the one in which Mahatma Gandhi briefly stayed in 1931 – hangs a portrait of him, wearing spectacles and a white home-spun cotton cloth and intently spinning on his simple wooden wheel. Downstairs, in the library, hangs a portrait of 'Quaker-Gandhian', Marjorie Sykes, radiant and focused, as I remember her both in India and on one of my visits to Woodbrooke. Past my window goes the traffic on the Bristol Road.

Cocooned in warm, creative silence I do not see the faces of those driving past, people as culturally diverse and individually plural, no doubt, as anywhere in the world. As an interfaith pilgrim I will soon be back on the bus, greeting the Sikh driver;

back at home in my Hindu family; back at work responding to students from many countries, and listening to my many other diverse neighbours.

As interfaith pilgrims we will be tasting and testing and we will ourselves be tested. We may glimpse something of truth, even the ineffable 'dazzling darkness' (to quote the poet Henry Vaughan). Or we may not. As we face towards the truth we will also be making it, through engaged, loving service of our neighbours. Faithfulness does not mean that we will all see or articulate truth in the same way or in the same place. The words which we use may sound too secular, too Christian or too unfamiliar to fellow Friends. We will respond to images and make some our own. In the shared silence, the unifying light, the differences disappear. We come to trust. We are little children; we have no labels. Our Quaker community provides us with a book of discipline, with inspiration for our journeying – much of it from its Christian past and its testimony to truth – and with loving support and companionship as we venture forth.

QUESTIONS FOR DISCUSSION

CHAPTER ONE

❀ Is our world really so different from the world of previous generations?

❀ Why should this require us to reconsider the question of what ultimate truth is?

❀ Am I spiritually plural? What terms would I use to describe this state?

❀ What elements can I detect in my own spirituality? (eg influences, treasured quotations, a film, experiences...)

❀ Is it really possible to be in 'dual membership' as far as faith is concerned?

CHAPTER TWO

❀ What do I know about interfaith initiatives locally? Nationally?

❀ How important are these? For social harmony? For developing an understanding of truth?

❀ What contacts have I had with people of other faiths?

❀ What jolts have these contacts given to how I see the world? (eg through our conversations, or through what I have noticed eg about worship or taboos)

❀ Do I stereotype neighbours from other communities? In what ways? How best can we leave the stereotypes behind?

CHAPTER THREE

❀ Is it helpful to examine my own conditioning?

❀ Is the Quaker aspect of me the most decisive in how I see things? What actually has more impact on my outlook?

❊ What does the emphasis of so many South Asians on using relationship words for people tell us about their understanding of society? How does this relate to 'religion'? Can we really separate religion and culture?

❊ Is Jesus messiah or guru for us today? Who else fills these roles? Do we need spiritual teachers, or are books, television and the internet enough?

❊ What have been my *sanskars* (in both the sense of conditioning and of life cycle rite)? Have other events been more decisive in making me what I am today?

CHAPTER FOUR

❊ Am I helped by any experiences that I have had of different ways of worshipping?

❊ How can the terms 'darshan', 'puja', 'arati' and 'mantra' set me thinking about how I worship?

❊ The lotus is one image among many. Which images from Christian, or any other, tradition, can bring me insight?

CHAPTER FIVE

❊ Is truth for me a matter of propositions or of gut feeling and intuition?

❊ In what ways is a clear statement of what is true useful for spiritual progress?

❊ Are God and Truth different words for the same thing (or state of being)?

❊ Are the beliefs which faiths share the most likely to be true?

❊ The Red Crescent and the Red Cross: is the fact that some individuals risk their lives to save others a valid indicator of the truth of their religious beliefs?

❊ Is exploring paradox a helpful way into grappling with what truth is?

CHAPTER SIX

❀ Discernment – when have I most felt in need of it? What most helped me to see the way forward?

❀ Is discerning the right course of action the same as discerning what is true? Does living truthfully require that we do both?

❀ When have I felt tested almost beyond my powers of endurance? What truth has come out of this for me? (It may be self-knowledge.)

❀ Love and risk-taking – does it make sense to look at my relationship with truth in these terms? What metaphor or analogy would work better for me in my journey towards truth?

GENERAL

❀ Is there any way in which reading any part of this book has been helpful (or unhelpful) on my own pilgrimage?

❀ Is there any way in which this book has added to my understanding of 'other faiths'?

FURTHER READING

All publications that have been mentioned in the text are listed below. Of particular interest may be Eck (1993), Hick (1999), Race (2001) and Singh (1995) as well as Knott, Kim (1998) *Hinduism: A Very Short Introduction*, Oxford: Oxford University Press.

REFERENCES

Adams, Tony (2000) 'Troth', *The Friend*, 19 May, 13.

Albright, Harry (1999) Editorial, *The Friend*, 29 January, 1.

Ali, Abdullah Yusuf (1946) *The Holy Qur'an: Text Translation and Commentary*, Qutar: Kamil Muslim Trust for Islamic Propagation Centre.

Ambler, Rex (2001) *Truth of the Heart – An Anthology of George Fox 1624-1691*, London: Quaker Books.

Armstrong, Karen (2000) *The Battle for God*, London: Random House.

Bailey, Sydney (1993) *Peace is a Process*, London: QHS.

Barnes, Michael (2000) 'Practising God's Hospitality', *World Faiths Encounter*, 27 (November), 12-16.

Boulter, Adam (no date) 'Journeying through Faith through Art' in Committee for Interfaith Concerns, *Friends in Truth: Some Examples of Good Practice in the Thames Valley Area*, Oxford: Committee for Interfaith Concerns, Diocese of Oxford, 75-76.

Bowker, Anne (no date) 'Interfaith Journey' in Committee for Interfaith Concerns [as above], 6-8.

Bowker, John (ed) (1997) *The Oxford Dictionary of World Religions*, Oxford: Oxford University Press.

Braybrooke, Marcus (1999) *Spiritual Experience that Crosses Religious Divisions*, Oxford: Oxford Religious Experience Research Centre, 2nd Series Occasional Paper 20.

Braybrooke, Marcus (2001) *Learn to Pray: A Practical Guide to Enriching your Life through Prayer*, London: Duncan Baird.

Braybrooke, Marcus (2002) in 'September 11th: One Year On', *One Family – The Newsletter of the World Congress of Faiths*, October, 3.

Britain Yearly Meeting (1995) *Quaker faith & practice*, London: The Yearly Meeting of the Religious Society of Friends (Quakers) in Britain.

Chidester, David (2000) *Christianity: A Global History*, Harmondsworth: Penguin.

Collins, Peter (1996) '"Plaining": The Social and Cognitive Practice of Symbolisation in the Religious Society of Friends (Quakers)', *Journal of Contemporary Religion*, 11 (3), 277-288.

Commission on British Muslims and Islamophobia (1997) *Islamophobia: A Challenge for Us All*, London: Runnymede Trust.

Copley, Terence (1998) *London Borough of Redbridge SACRE Annual Lecture*, Redbridge, SACRE, 21 October.

Cragg, Kenneth (1970) *Alive to God: Muslim and Christian Prayer*, Oxford: Oxford University Press.

Cragg, Kenneth (2nd ed) (1985) *The Call of the Minaret*, London: Collins.

Dart, Martha (1989) *To Meet at the Source: Hindus and Quakers*, Wallingford, PA: Pendle Hill Pamphlet.

DCosta, Gavin (2000) *The Meeting of Religions and the Trinity*, London: T. and T. Clark.

Dhingra, Leena (1988) *Amritvela*, London: Women's Press.

Doniger O'Flaherty, Wendy (1999) 'The Uses and Misuses of Other People's Myths', in Russell T. McCutcheon (ed)

119

The Insider/Outsider Problem in the Study of Religion A Reader, London: Cassell, 31-49.

Drabble, Margaret (1996) *The Witch of Exmoor*, Harmondsworth: Penguin.

Dutt, Leila (1984) *Rubik's Cube*, Denbigh: Gee and Son.

Eck, Diana (1993) *Encountering God: A Spiritual Journey from Bozeman to Banaras*, Boston: Beacon Press.

Esack, Farid (1997) *Qur'an Liberation and Pluralism: An Islamic Perspective of Interreligious Solidarity against Oppression*, Oxford: Oneworld.

Feldman, Christina (1994) *The Quest of the Warrior Woman: A Path of Healing, Empowerment and Transformation*, London: Aquarian.

Fernandez-Armesto, Felipe (1997) *Truth: A History and a Guide for the Perplexed*, London: Black Swan.

Ford, David (1999) *Self and Salvation: Being Transformed*, Cambridge: Cambridge University Press.

Freeman, Lawrence (2000) *Jesus the Teacher Within*, New York: Continuum.

Gandhi, Mohandas Karamchand (1927) *The Story of My Experiments with Truth*, Ahmedabad: Navajivan Publishing House.

Gandhi, Mohandas Karamchand (1928) *Satyagraha in South Africa*, Ganesan: Madras.

Gunward, Larry (2002) 'Buddhism Quakerism', *The Friend*, 20 September, 6.

Gwyn, Douglas (1989) *Unmasking the Idols – A Journey among Friends*, Richmond, Indiana: Friends United Press.

Gwyn, Douglas (1989-1997) *Words in Time: Essays and Addresses*, Bellefonte, Pennsylvania: Kimo Press.

Hick, John (1990) 'A Philosophy of Religious Pluralism' in Paul Badham (ed) *A John Hick Reader*, London: Macmillan, 161-177.

Hick, John (1995) *The Rainbow of Faiths*, London: SCM.

Hick, John (1999) *The Fifth Dimension: An Exploration of the Spiritual World*, Oxford: Oneworld.

Hooker, Roger (1973) *Uncharted Journey*, London: Church Missionary Society.

Huber, Klaus (2001) 'Questions of Identity among "Buddhist Quakers"', *Quaker Studies*, 6 (1) 80-105.

Huebner, Dwayne (1993) 'Education and Spirituality', *Journal for Curriculum Theory*, 3, 13-34.

Hull, John (1991) *Mishmash: Religious Education in Multi-Cultural Britain, A Study in Metaphor*, Birmingham: The University of Birmingham and the Christian Education Movement.

Huntington, S.P. (1996) *The Clash of Civilizations and the Remaking of World Order*, New York: Simon and Schuster.

Ipgrave, Julia (2001) *Pupil-to-Pupil – Dialogue in the Classroom as a Tool for Religious Education*, Coventry: Warwick Religions and Education Research Unit, Institute of Education, University of Warwick.

Jackson, Robert (1989) *Religions through Festivals: Hinduism*, London: Longman.

Jackson, Robert and Killingley, Dermot (1988) *Approaches to Hinduism*, London: John Murray.

Jackson, Robert and Nesbitt, Eleanor (1993) *Hindu Children in Britain*, Stoke-on-Trent: Trentham.

Loring, Patricia (1992) *Spiritual Discernment: The Context and Goal of Clearness Committees*, Wallingford, PA: Pendle Hill.

Mascaro, Juan (1965) (trans) *The Upanishads*, Harmondsworth: Penguin.

Maw, Geoffrey (1997) *Pilgrims in Hindu Holy Land: Sacred Shrines of the Indian Himalayas* (eds Gillian M. Conacher and Marjorie Sykes), York: Sessions.

Maw, Geoffrey (no date) *Narmada, The Life of a River* (ed Marjorie Sykes), Hoshangabad: Friends Rural Centre.

McIntosh, Alistair (2000) 'God in All Creation', *Quaker monthly* 79 (2), 163-167.

McLeod, W. Hew (1980) *The B40 Janam-Sakhi: An English*

Translation with Introduction and Annotation of India Office Library Gurmukhi Manuscript Panj. B40. A Janam-Sakhi of Guru Nanak Compiled in A.D. 1733, Amritsar: Guru Nanak Dev University.

Morgan, Peggy (1989) 'Worship and the Example of Buddhism' in Angela Wood (1989) *Religions and Education*, Isleworth: BFSS National RE Centre.

Murdoch, Iris (1983) *The Philosopher's Pupil*, London: Penguin.

Nesbitt, Eleanor (1999a) 'Friend in the Field: A Reflexive Approach to Being a Quaker Ethnographer', *Quaker Studies*, 4 (2), 82-112.

Nesbitt, Eleanor (1999b) '"Being Religious Shows in your Food": Young British Hindus and Vegetarianism' in T.S. Rukmani (ed) *Hindu Diaspora: Global Perspectives*, Montreal: Chair in Hindu Studies, Concordia University, 397-426.

Nesbitt, Eleanor (1999c) *Turn But a Stone*, Norwich: Hilton House.

Nesbitt, Eleanor (2000) *The Religious Lives of Sikh Children: A Coventry Based Study*, Leeds: Community Religions Project, University of Leeds.

Nesbitt, Eleanor and Kaur, Gopinder (1999) *Guru Nanak*, Norwich: Religious and Moral Education Press.

Northern Friends Peace Board (1997) *Who Am I? Who Are You? Views of National Identity in Britain*, Bolton: Northern Friends Peace Board.

Palmer, Parker (1998) *The Courage to Teach: Exploring the Inner Landscape of a Teacher's Life*, San Francisco: Jossey-Bass Publishers.

Panikkar, Raimon (1978) *Interreligious Dialogue*, New York: Paulist Press.

Parker-Rhodes, Damaris (1977) *Truth: A Path not a Possession* (Swarthmore Lecture 1977), London: Quaker Home Service.

Patel, K. Swaminathan (1988) *A Gandhi Reader*, Madras: Orient Longman.

Potter, Jean and Braybrooke, Marcus (eds) (1997) *All in Good Faith: A Resource Book for Multi-Faith Prayer*, Oxford: The World Congress of Faiths.

Premchand (no date) *Mansarovar*, Allahabad: Saraswati Press [Hindi].

Punshon, John (1984, rev. rpt. 2001) *Portrait in Grey – A Short History of the Quakers*, London: Quaker Books.

Punshon, John (1987) *Encounter with Silence*, London: Quaker Home Service.

Punshon, John (1990) *Testimony and Tradition – Some Aspects of Quaker Spirituality*, London: Quaker Home Service.

Pym, Jim (1999) *Listening to Light: How to Bring Quaker Simplicity and Integrity into Our Lives*, London: Rider.

Pym, Jim (2000) *The Pure Principle: Quakers and Other Faiths*, York: William Sessions.

Race, Alan (2001) *Interfaith Encounter*, London: SCM Press.

Robinson, Francis (1996) 'Knowledge, Its Transmission, and the Making of Muslim Societies' in Francis Robinson (ed) *The Cambridge Illustrated History of the Islamic World*, Cambridge: Cambridge University Press, 208-249.

Rudge, Linda (1998) '"I Am Nothing" – Does it Matter? A Critique of Current Religious Education Policy and Practice in England on behalf of the Silent Majority', *British Journal of Religious Education*, 20 (3), 155-165.

Runnymede Commission on Antisemitism (rep. 1997) *A Very Light Sleeper: The Persistence and Dangers of Antisemitism*, London: Runnymede Trust.

Sacks, Jonathan (2002) *The Dignity of Difference: How to Avoid the Clash of Civilizations*, London: Continuum.

Said, Edward (1985) *Orientalism*, Harmondsworth: Penguin.

St. Ruth, Richard and St. Ruth, Diana (comp) (1997) *The Little Book of Buddhist Wisdom*, Shaftesbury: Element.

Schindler, Alexander M. (1988) 'Introduction' in Daniel B.

Syme *The Jewish Home A Guide for Jewish Living*, New York: UAHC Press.

Singh, Nikky-Guninder Kaur (1995) *The Name of My Beloved: Verses of the Sikh Gurus*, San Francisco: HarperCollins.

Smart, Ninian (1989) *The World's Religions*, Cambridge: Cambridge University Press.

Tennyson, Margot (1998) *Millennium Interfaith Invocation Universal Love*, Birmingham: The Leaveners (Quaker Community Arts Project).

Thangaraj, M. Thomas (1994) *The Crucified Guru: An Experiment in Cross-Cultural Christology*, Nashville: Abingdon.

Vallely, Paul (2002) 'Carey leaves behind a big question', *The Independent*, Jan 8, 5.

Vaudeville, Charlotte (1974) *Kabir Volume 1*, Oxford: Oxford University Press.

Voas, David (forthcoming 2003) 'Intermarriage and the Demography of Secularisation', *British Journal of Sociology*.

Ward, Keith (2000) 'Convergent Spirituality' in Deborah A. Brown (ed) *Christianity in the Twenty-First Century*, New York: Crossroads, 41-71.

Weller, Paul (ed) (2001) *Religions in the UK: Directory 2001-03*, Derby: the Multi-Faith Centre at the University of Derby in association with the Inter Faith Network for the United Kingdom.

Wildwood, Alex (1999) *A Faith to Call our Own: Quaker Tradition in the Light of Contemporary Movements of the Spirit*, London: Quaker Home Service.

Williams, Rowan (2000) *On Christian Theology*, Oxford: Blackwell.

Zimmer, Heinrich (1946) *Myths and Symbols in Indian Art and Civilisation*, New York: Pantheon Books.